Serena's Serenity

Lisa Moravek

Psalm 26:7—"That I may publish with the voice of thanksgiving, and tell of all thy wondrous works."

DayStarPublishing
Post Office Box 464
Miamitown, Ohio 45041
1-800-311-1823
www.daystarpublishing.org

Cover design: Judith Moravek

Published by DayStar Publishing
Post Office Box 464
Miamitown, Ohio 45041

Printed in the United States of America
by Bible and Missionary Literature
713 South Cannon Boulevard
Shelbyville, Tennessee 37160

**Library of Congress Cataloging-in-Publication
Data**
Library of Congress control number - 2010925569

Moravek, Lisa, 1977-
Serena's Serenity.

ISBN: 978-1-890120-71-9

Dedication

Sincere gratitude to those who listened and helped to bear my burdens in various ways...especially to my parents who had us as residents for a while, and Theola who is my "Jerusha." May I be that "someone" for others.

Thank you to the real-life Huff family who are modern examples of meekness, like Moses in the Old Testament, who search their own hearts first and are careful to give others the benefit of the doubt.

I appreciate my pastors over the years who have preached God's Word faithfully and for their wives.

Most of all, my praise goes to God Who gave me the greatest Comforter of all, the Holy Spirit, found by trusting Jesus Christ as my Saviour. He brings us <u>through</u> our valleys.

Verses from His Word that have greatly encouraged me...
I Corinthians 10:31b—"whatsoever ye do, do all to the glory of God."
Galatians 1:10—"For do I now persuade men, or God? or do I seek to please men? for if I yet pleased men, I should not be the servant of Christ."

Meet **Lisa Moravek**...

Lisa is married to a loving, devoted husband who has faithfully worked two jobs for years so that she may stay home and instruct their five children. Their sixth baby was an identical twin that they lost at thirty-six weeks due to a cord accident. God has brought them through many difficult trials that make her writing believable. She completed a writing course through the Institute of Children's Literature in 1997. Then she co-authored a biography for friends entitled *Joy in the Mourning* that they self-published in 2002. Lisa has taught private piano lessons for eighteen years. For over a year now, she's been teaching at Fletcher's School of Music in Horseheads, New York, three evenings a week to allow her husband Dennis some time with the children. Lisa deeply respects her parents who sacrificed to home educate her and her sisters.

Meet **Judith Moravek,** illustrator...

Judith, Lisa's mother-in-"love", has been married to her husband Alan for forty years. She was supportive as he pastored for fourteen and a half years in New York State and has been by his side as they've traveled in evangelism for eighteen years. Judith is very artistic and has also written poetry and composed Christian songs.

PROLOGUE

Perhaps you are a stay at home mom, in the midst of doldrums... You perform day-in and day-out the continuous cycle of housework, teaching, tending to sick children, unplanned doctor visits, little sleep and possibly limited time with your husband for whom you try to stay attractive and interesting. By "journeying" with Serena, may you appreciate what you have more than ever and realize that the sometimes glamorous career life isn't all it seems. May your sufficiency be of God Who is able to make all grace abound toward you. Proverbs 11:30 states that he that winneth souls is wise. Lisa yearns for this novel to boost your morale to continue winning your children's souls one day at a time. Enjoy this season of your life to the fullest!

Main Characters' Profiles

Serena Callahan: the main character who loves the Lord and is trying to balance being a loving wife, working outside the home, and endeavoring to reunite with her children

Carl Callahan: Serena's Godly, grieving husband who is trying his best to provide for the family

Allegra: Serena and Carl's eight year old daughter

Brookelle and Joelle: their six year old twins who had to be sent to live with Serena's parents in New York State

Emili Huff: Serena's employer

Mr. Huff: Emili's husband

Blaire and Claire: the Huffs' twins and Serena's charges

Jerusha Kenaston: Serena's dear friend that she met at a laundromat in Ohio

Bethany Jasmine: Serena's home schooled childhood friend from New York who is now a doctor

Dan and Barb: the groundskeeper and housekeeper that live on the Huffs' premises

Stephen Eclant: the pastor's son and church pianist as well as friend to the Callahans

Main Characters' Profiles

Suzanne Patton and her family: home schooling friends from church

Dominic and Merry Victor: missionary friends from church   Merry had been Serena's first piano student in Ohio and had become like a sister.

Jim: the Callahans' neighbor on the dirty street in Dayton, Ohio

Mr. Shelby: Carl's coworker who donated a cemetery plot

Timmy, Chuck and Alice Barletta: New York church members and Brookelle and Joelle's Sunday school teacher

Chapter One

The Nanny Position

The gentle sunlight that filtered down through the various leaves and landed quietly to warm the shady grass didn't cause Serena's heart to rejoice like usual. Normally, Serena took deep breaths on days like this one...as if basking her very soul in God's goodness. She always enjoyed finding reasons to be outdoors or to run errands in such weather.

How eight-year-old Allegra had delighted in car rides on these types of days, too. They'd choose back routes to the Post Office or store, so they could take their time and study the clouds. Serena had enjoyed science class even as an elementary student. She was fascinated by the many formations and would recite them to herself while swinging at recess. The chains were long; and she'd pump her legs until she was smoothly soaring into the sky, the wind blowing and tugging at her brown hair.

Allegra retained factual information with ease like her daddy, and she would exclaim in a pleased sort of way..."Those are cirrus clouds because they are feathery like a circus clown's hat feathers. Right, Mommy?"

"Absolutely!" Serena affirmed, as she'd reach out to squeeze her hand. "Who made you so smart?"

"God!" Allegra responded with a fervor that matched her name.

"Allegra means vivacious and lively," Serena remembered having told the nurse when she was born.

But she's not here, Serena thought. *I know; I know! Stop reminding me,* she silently scolded herself. The familiar feeling of claustrophobia began to creep in close. The old, foreign-made car seemed smaller than ever. A sudden curve in the road jarred her from the suffocating grief temporarily. Serena forced herself to concentrate on the task at hand. She glanced down at the index card propped up in the pen slot of the console between the front seats. Her scribbled writing read *48 Maple Drive.* The street was beginning to incline as it gradually wound to the right.

"How odd for Ohio, " she murmured to herself. Having been born and reared in New York's Southern Tier, she was accustomed to large tree-covered hills that hid the roads and houses from the highway...at least all summer long. Here in southwestern Ohio, the topography was flat like she envisioned Iowa and other farming states to be. Traveling home to visit was always a bore the first half of the trip. Ohio's interstate was well maintained with smooth blacktop. Serena would always stock up on library books to read aloud to Allegra and the six year old twins at intervals over the course of the first four and a half hours. Carl, her loving husband and devoted father to the girls, would interject humor or quiz the girls on what they had heard while he drove.

"My dear," Serena would say jovially-- interrupting his pop comprehension tests, "you know full well that our girls can answer all of your questions since they have memories like yours."

"Is that so?" Carl would tease, a smile showing milky white teeth beneath his trimmed, black moustache.

Once they reached Pennsylvania, it took another hour and a half to pass the large sign welcoming them to New York. Serena's eyes always feasted on the rolling view. The rough highway was comforting somehow. The tires seemed to drone words to Serena as the rubber bumped over the cement sections every half-second or so. "You're back; you're back. Welcome home; welcome home."

Here and now, Serena strained her eyes to read the numbers on the well-maintained mailboxes. Freshly mulched flower beds adorned the yards that were of golf course perfection. Serena was not a gardener; but, to her, the nameless plants were jewels of color amidst the leafy arbors the tree branches created as they stretched to touch each other.

How fun it would be to park and meander through the yards and woodsy vacant lots with her girls. Doctor Stiles had advised her to concentrate on the little things, but how would she ever find time? The miniature forests appeared to have been planted and cared for by professional landscapers. Several young trees were staked, and there were no visible patches of last year's leaf accumulation on the ground.

The sprawling homes had privacy from each other, and most were set back and uphill from the paved road. Serena could only catch glimpses of the mansions around the calculated plantings. She passed a mailbox with bronze numbers attached to its wooden post. "Number thirty-six. Six more houses to go on the right side," she said with a heavy sigh.

Her palms felt sweaty as she gripped the steering wheel. A spotless candy apple red sports utility vehicle was coming down the road. Serena felt out of place driving her rusty white clunker in this elite neighborhood. The driver was a woman dressed in a tailored suit and wearing sunglasses. Staring straight ahead, Serena avoided making direct eye contact when they passed each other-- though she forced herself to smile pleasantly. She hoped the stranger would take notice that, despite the car's year and decay, it was shiny clean.

Then she spotted the bold numbers affirming her destination. She slowly turned right again. The meticulous lawn was like a velvety carpet, its plush ness cut evenly at the sides of the long brick driveway. Serena thought about the dandelion leaves she would pick at their old house in the mornings and stash in the 'fridge for salads.

The...what family lived at this residence? Serena referred to the three and a half by five-inch card again. *Oh, yes. The Huff family. Well, they can't provide a healthy salad for themselves whenever they desire--free of charge.*

Serena knew she'd enjoy the beauty of such a yard, but she tried to console herself that she and Carl did the best they could. Their lives were filled with priorities that couldn't be rearranged. Besides, how many women would care to rise early before the weed flowers' blossoms opened to select the crispest leaves to save grocery money? She wasn't poor due to lack of enterprise. She was whom God had made her to be, and she would try not to feel intimidated.

Reaching the top of the drive, she carefully parked where Mrs. Kenaston, her friend at the Laundromat, had instructed. She had been so absorbed in her thoughts about the yard that she realized she hadn't taken notice of the house. She peered into the rear view mirror so as not to appear overly curious should someone be watching her. Serena inhaled deeply as she nervously viewed the exterior of the home that reminded her of the glowing paintings in the art gallery at the mall. The recessed back door alcove appeared to be brick. The siding was ordinary white with black shutters framing the clean windows that reflected the newly green trees beside the house.

An older man came around the opposite end of the house--power washing the siding. Serena sat taller in her seat and briefly checked her lipstick and eye makeup in the rear view mirror. Having suffered with allergies since she was a child, the springtime eye and ear itching was nothing new but still an irritation nonetheless. Her non-drowsy medicine was gone, and there wasn't enough money to buy more for a few weeks at least. She tried to alleviate the insatiable itch by pressing the sides of her fingers against her eyes.

No matter how gentle she tried to be, her moderately applied eyeliner always seemed to smudge. Serena grabbed a tissue from the box in the console and rubbed off the smudged makeup.

Grasping her purse, she opened the door. Undoubtedly the elderly man would assure her that she was going to the proper entrance or hopefully show her in. She shut the car door firmly to alert the man of her presence without startling him. The man looked spry enough, but she never was good at guessing people's ages.

Her gently worn, second-hand sandals clicked on the brick sidewalk, which was exactly like the driveway only narrower. She mustered up what she prayed would be interpreted as a confident air. How grateful she'd be if this Mrs. Emili Huff would perceive her as determined to work hard. Just an opportunity to prove her character would be enough. She couldn't let this woman with the harsh sounding name fluster her. Would she be large boned and solid the way her name sounded?

Serena approached the man eagerly, ignoring the cleaning solution that misted her as the forceful spray hit the vinyl. "Excuse me, sir!" she called out. He continued staring directly ahead, moving his hand back and forth as he pointed the nozzle several inches lower with each sweep. Serena raised her voice louder. "Sir, excuse me, please!"

The man seemed rooted where he was. He worked at a steady pace, oblivious to her. Serena hesitated. The back door was just four feet from this stranger. Usually Serena could get along with anybody. Mother had always said that she was her peace-loving child.

Glancing at her cheap watch, the hands revealed that she was now one minute late. She forced herself to run through the sprinkle-filled air toward the bright red door adorned with a wreath of artificial seasonal leaves, vines, and blossoms. Hurriedly she lifted the heavy brass knocker handle. It clacked against the metal plate that was screwed discreetly to the solid door. It opened promptly.

"You are nine minutes early. That's good." A small-boned woman, who looked almost frail, motioned her into a large, airy kitchen. Serena took a deep, silent breath, relieved to remember that her watch was set ten minutes fast.

The petite lady pulled out a wooden chair for Serena before sitting down herself. The honey-tone stained chairs were a cheery contrast against the spotless glazed white porcelain tabletop. A navy blue serving bowl heaped with luscious, bright red strawberries attracted the eyes.

"As you know," the woman began hurriedly, "my name is Emili. Mrs. Kenaston, our neighbors' housekeeper, informed us that she met you at the Laundromat near her apartment. Please don't misunderstand the following questions, but a mother can never be too careful in protecting her children."

Suddenly Emili stood up and pushed back the chair with her legs. She ran and slid across the glossy linoleum and firmly closed the window over the sink. "We can't have Dan showering this entire room!" Her butterfly sleeves fluttered as she dropped back into her seat then fell to rest against her thin arms. The delicate material of the blouse enhanced her figure by softening her protruding elbows and wrist bones. "Now," the lady continued, "what is your name?"

"Serena Callahan, Mrs. Huff."

"Miss Emili suits me just fine, Serena. Do you have a reliable car to come and go dependably five and a half days out of each week?" Emili's brown eyes were piercing. They were so dark that Serena barely noticed her pupils.

Serena felt as if the intense stare could decipher all her thoughts. She swallowed, trying not to portray her increasing awkwardness around this fast-paced woman. How she longed to be home caring for her three precious children. Instead she was interviewing for a job that would have no end in sight with a woman whose name matched her personality. Serena found herself wishing that this lady were huffier in build than curt in tongue.

"Well?" Emili asked impatiently.

"Yes, Miss Emili," Serena managed to choke out around the salty tears she tasted in the back of her throat that stung her sinuses. She knew she couldn't afford to lose all her confidence, especially when becoming a family again depended on this job.

"Great," she said without a smile. Proceeding in her strictly business manner, she queried, "Are you married, do you have children, or are you planning on starting a family soon?"

Serena moistened her lips. "I've been married to Carl for nine years, but you needn't concern yourself with children disrupting my work. I came prepared with three references should you desire to see my list. Work is our top priority for a while," she concluded in the most cheerful tone she could muster.

"How refreshing!" Emili gushed. "Two girls have already left my employ to ruin their lives by marrying young. I worked six days a week and attended night classes for several years. Then...*then*, mind you, I said 'yes' to my successful husband. We heed the Golden Rule and assist various local charities, and circumstances work out well for us." She ran her fingers through her thick, straight brown hair. The shoulder-length strands glistened here and there with sunny highlights…the modern fresh spring look.

Serena heard pounding water and turned to see it cascading down the closed window. Emili stated, "Dan and his wife Barb are the hardest workers we've ever had in our employ. It's our goal to succeed with hiring more diligent help."

Serena crossed her right foot over her left ankle beneath the table and silently prayed that she wouldn't ask any more questions. *Please, God, You know how badly I need this job.*

Emili reached toward the five and a half by seven inch red frame that was on a nearby countertop. She picked it up and, while turning it around, set it in front of Serena. Healthy twin girls stared up from the studio portrait. They were dressed in matching Christmas dresses with hats contrasting each other's. Having stunning blue eyes that Serena assumed they inherited from their father, they still favored Emili due to their distinct piercing gazes and brown hair.

Emili spoke as she stood. "Since Mrs. Kenaston referred you, and she's been a trustworthy employee for our neighbor Andrea for two years, I see no need to question you further. Barb will give you a tour of the house in the morning. Be here at seven."

Serena was relieved not to cross paths with Dan on her way out. Now that the dreaded initial meeting was over, her legs felt like jelly. It felt so good to climb into her familiar car. She decided to make the most of today and visit Allegra's grave since it might be a while before she'd have an opportunity to drive out there again.

Carefully she backed up in the turn-around then followed the driveway to the street. If only she had thought to ask Mrs. Kenaston which neighboring house she worked in. Still, it was comforting to know that someone kind would be nearby each day.

Serena thanked God for the new job, but her pleasure in the crisp spring day had evaporated into the bright rays of sunshine that glinted off the hood of the car. She stared at the road as she departed from that horrid luxury and woman exemplar. Serena sensed that Miss Emili fancied herself to be a model of morals and propriety for all poor human creatures that would—rather *should*— take notice. The Ohioan title "Miss" for married women was a different usage than Serena had learned in New York. At the age of twelve, Serena had passed a Red Cross course on childcare and safety and became a licensed babysitter. Her little charges had called her Miss 'Rena. After living in the suburbs of Dayton since the wedding, she still puzzled over calling someone "Miss" who was really a "Mrs.".

Still a mystery, too, was the strange looks cashiers gave her in the stores. "Where are you from?" they'd be sure to ask.

Serena would smile politely. "New York. It's amazing how 'ya'll' can notice my accent when I've only said 'Hello' and 'Yes, plastic bags please. How is your day going?'"

The store employees would always chuckle at her southern "ya'll" that imitated their southern drawl they prided themselves in. She reminded herself that, living in Fairborn, she was among many college students from Wright State University as well as airmen and women from all over— stationed at Wright Patterson Air Force Base. Maybe it kept life interesting for the workers to tally how many States, even countries, would be represented by customers like herself during one of their shifts. She asked Carl, when they were newlyweds, why even the pastor referred to New Yorkers as "Yankees." "Ohioans were on the Union's side in the Civil War as well. They're Yankees just as much as we are. I can't figure it."

Carl only answered by squeezing her shoulder. "I just know that I love you, and don't forget that I'm from New York, too."

Serena wished they could live in New York State right this moment to be near her girls. Then she could visit them each day after work.

14

Somehow she found herself at the old cemetery beside a church. She parked the car beside the deserted country road. With spade and cup in hand, she walked back into the overgrown grounds. Nestled in the center of taller monuments was a newer grave with a small headstone that angled slightly upward. Kneeling down, Serena rubbed her hands over the damp earth. She remembered what it felt like to pat her energetic daughter's healthy arms when she had been sweaty but was resting in a cool breeze.

"Oh, Allegra! Allegra!" she sobbed, burying her face against her dirty hands. "Please, God, let me die, too. I can't bear life without our opinionated, challenging child." The tears flowed until Serena felt spent and empty. The numbness felt good after the stressful interview. This new pressure was too soon. The world was harshly pushing her onward. A few days to mourn weren't enough.

She stood up before brushing at her wet face with her sleeves. Carelessly she fingered her straying, wispy bangs back into her long hair. Allegra must have flowers on her grave. The small number of florists' arrangements that had been brought from the funeral home was brown and depressing. Serena picked her way through the overgrowth toward the open field beyond the cemetery.

A startled milk snake shinnied away from her feet deeper into the waist-high weeds. As she waded into them herself, she cried out as she felt a sharp jab on her leg. Expecting to see another snake, she was relieved when she discovered a burr clinging to her stockings at her ankle. "You should have known better," she scolded herself. "Your last pair of hose that needed to last at least another week." Carefully working it loose with her slender fingers still produced a small hole and a run that sped toward her big toe.

Inhaling deeply before letting her breath out with a sigh, Serena tossed the tiny organic ball across the top of the waving grasses. At that moment, the soothing breeze paused for a rest, so the cotton-weight burr's flight didn't take it as far as Serena had desired. She watched, as the little hitchhiker seemed to parachute for a gentle landing on the weeds' purple blossoms.

"Allegra's worth wearing socks for...all week, while I work. Attending church with socks on will be more humiliating," Serena mused aloud to the chattering birds. Grasping her small garden spade with more determination, she hunted for the loveliest wildflowers she could find.

The safety orange, glowing sun was level with her sensitive blue eyes as she finally headed back toward the grave with an armload of flowers, roots dangling. Serena dropped her hiked-up skirt for the third time to swipe at the stringy hair that clung to her sweaty forehead. There was no need to rush home to make supper for Carl. He'd be out applying for a second part-time job. Serena dug deep holes that the roots could dangle into. Joelle and Brookelle would have loved to be helping her.

Using her travel cup, she visited the creek several yards away. After several trips, she had amply drenched each hole before easing the delicate roots down in. She sifted the earth on top of them until the holes were filled in then firmly pressed the remaining loose dirt into mounds around the stems. She lightly watered the troweled ground until she was satisfied that the free flowers wouldn't go into shock from thirst after the day's trauma. The sky was dusky as she stiffly tottered to her feet to survey the transplants. Their daughter's grave, as well as the one beside it, showed no traces of weeds. The hardy wildflowers already stood proudly in front of both monuments.

Serena clapped the dirt from her hands then brushed at her skirt before opening the car door. She set her dirty spade and cup gingerly on the floor in the back. As she pulled out onto the quiet road, she looked ahead at the open sky and the faint feathery clouds tinted dark red that merged into the growing inky blue. Carl's coworker, Mr. Shelby, would be pleased if he were to visit his first wife's grave. She had passed away thirty-five years ago, and he had remarried three years later. When the explosion had... Well, when Allegra suddenly needed to be buried, this kind man had generously given them the shared plot he had purchased for himself long ago. Since he and his first wife hadn't had children, his present family couldn't think of his being buried in the forlorn place rather than beside "Mom."

After merging onto the highway, Serena finally exited onto one of Dayton's inner city ramps. She took a deep, shaky breath as she turned onto her littered street. People hung out lazily on their ramshackled porches, their cigarettes lighting the evening like diseased fireflies. She hoped the neighbor below Carl's and her apartment wouldn't be on his front steps. He unnerved her when he stared with his hardened eyes. Whenever she tried to be formally polite and called out a brave-sounding "Hello," he'd just shift his eyes.

After parallel parking as close to the apartment as possible, she noticed that the upstairs windows were still dark. Several cars whizzed by in quick succession, their rock music thumping so loudly that it vibrated her car. Serena searched in her rear view mirror and through the windshield for a glimpse of Carl's small pickup truck. "If only I had left some lights on this morning," she fretted. Then she noticed their neighbor settled comfortably on his porch. She nodded quickly as she endeavored to pass by him briskly on the sidewalk toward the enclosed back steps. She grimaced as he called after her. "You need to utilize your mirrors. Looking over your shoulders will mess you up every time."

Without turning all the way around, she mustered a pleasant, "Thank you. I'll keep that in mind." She was amazed that this man spoke perfect English. Hurrying on toward the door, she dreaded climbing the L-shaped staircase alone after having been gone all day. The divided, rambling house was so old that there was no light switch just inside the locked door. She'd have to climb several steps, turn and mount the last few before reaching the inside door and the light switch.

From now on, she'd leave several lights on even if she planned to be home before dark. This place didn't feel or smell like home yet. She doubted if it ever would without her being home every day to clean—and especially without her three children's chatter filling every corner. Would life ever be normal again? Serena fiddled with the key in the darkness. Finally the door swung in, and she managed to shut it behind her with her foot.

Her heart pounded against her ribs. She stood still as she evaluated the situation. Now she had to conquer her fear of the upper half of the entrance as well as the foreboding apartment. She was concentrating so hard on the silence that she began to hear buzzing in her ears. Deciding against locking the door in case she needed to make a hasty retreat, she began to tiptoe. She felt for the firm wood on the step above before resting all her weight to ascend to the next. *Fear not, for I am with thee,* Serena thought over and over again as she rounded the corner.

Holding her breath, she felt the dirty wall with her outstretched left hand as she balanced her things in her right arm. Peeling paint chipped off and wedged under her fingernails. She bumped the switch with her palm and flicked it on vigorously with all five fingers. As the lone thirty-five watt light bulb shone down on her, a bang sounded on the other side of the apartment door.

Serena fled back down, dropping her armload in the process. She reached the outside door just as someone was opening it. Serena slammed into it with all her weight, fighting to lock the handle as she leaned her shoulders hard against the solid wood. She kept looking behind her. Surely the upstairs was harboring some hoodlum, and now the loafing neighbor was attempting to break in. She was relieved that the doors didn't have windows.

"Serena!" shouted a familiar voice. "Why aren't you letting me in? What's going on?"

She collapsed onto the bottom step, suddenly feeling paralyzing numbness take the place of her adrenalin rush. Carl unlocked the knob once again. He left the door open to kneel on the floor below her. Serena slumped into his arms, and he caught her as she gasped for air. She pressed against his strong body and whispered, "I must have been holding my breath. I heard a bang that sounded like an inflated plastic shopping bag being popped in the kitchen."

"Stay here," Carl instructed in a hushed voice. "If I yell to you, race for the car and go to the shopping center."

Serena strained to hear every creak that came from the floors above. Finally, she heard him quietly call her. "Serena, it's safe to come up." Then she saw his brown eyes searching for her around the stairwell's turn. She began picking up her scattered belongings. Carl skipped two steps at a time to help. Serena stood where she was until he had locked the outside door and was coming back up with his lunch box as well. Reluctantly, she led the way; but Carl spoke softly, "I'll go first."

Once they were in the kitchen, Carl shut and locked the kitchen door. "I think you must have heard Jim working around in his apartment. I searched thoroughly."

"Behind the futon and in the shower?" Serena confirmed.

"Yes." Carl made earnest eye contact before wrapping his arms around her reassuringly.

"Thank you," Serena murmured, content to rest her head beneath his chin.

"Have you eaten yet?" Carl spoke against her hair.

"No."

"I'll do the honors and cook up some grilled cheese sandwiches if you don't mind putting on some decaf coffee. Then we can eat together on the futon."

"Sounds good. I need to wind down before I'll be able to sleep."

Carl promptly washed his hands and set to work rummaging in the half-settled cupboards and half-empty boxes for the griddle while Serena asked, "How did you know the tenant below us is named Jim?"

"I met him today when I left for work."

Serena's feet ached. She longed to slip off her shoes, but the thought of walking on the soiled carpets unprotected from the previous resident's germs hindered her. She kept shifting her weight, attempting to relieve some of the throbbing in her legs. Her doctor had called her the varicosity queen when she was expecting the twins. Her condition was also genetic since her grandmother had weak veins.

Once the sandwiches were browned, and Serena had poured the steaming black coffee for herself and had stirred two teaspoons of sugar into Carl's, they walked carefully into the living area. "Ah," Serena exhaled as she eased onto the clean futon that they had purchased with the love offering from church. Carl set his plate and mug on a kitchen chair he had brought to double as a coffee table then leaned down to kiss her on the forehead.

"I'm sorry for your sake that we must live here, Honey." He held her gaze in deep sincerity. "I'm glad I got home when I did."

Serena stared at him, willing the moment to last. Carl was always the perfect gentleman, but he kept her guessing as to when he'd be romantic. She cuddled up against his arm when he sat down beside her. "Let's pray," he said, squeezing her hand.

Chapter Two

Joelle and Brookelle

Serena's heart was so warmed by Carl's tender affection that she slept peacefully beside him for the first time since Allegra's death and the twins' departure to New York with her parents. Her nerves were soothed enough that she didn't seem to notice the wooden slats beneath the futon's mattress. Somehow the morning light made the new job more appealing, especially since she'd be escaping the stale, smoky smell that permeated from the old carpets.

Since she wasn't much of a conversationalist, Serena was relieved when Mrs. Huff drove away. The large house was still quiet, and Serena rubbed her foot back and forth on the smooth dining room floor. Her clean sock glided across its surface. The cleanliness felt refreshing and familiar. As she inhaled deeply of the home's fresh smelling air, she surveyed the surroundings more keenly than she had in Miss Emili's presence. Her new employer had said that the twins shouldn't wake up for another hour, so Serena decided to look around.

Picking up the schedule off the table, she cautiously explored each room. Fresh vacuum marks inhibited her from walking too far into each room since her footprints would show. She was unsure when the housekeeper would arrive, and she'd hate being caught in any off-limit rooms. She would have to ask her or the girls about the house rules though she didn't remember Miss Emili mentioning any.

She walked down the hall toward the front of the house. The spacious entry was tiled with beige ceramic that complemented the pink-toned marble floor in the adjoining company sitting room. Serena assumed that the marble allowed for visitors' shoes year-round. The parlor was paneled with cherry wood and adorned with subtle wall lighting that enhanced the glossy hue, making the large room seem homier. A soft area rug was situated at an angle toward the far corner that drew her attention to a realistic gas fireplace. A wispy dried flower arrangement sat on the large mantle adding gentleness to the rich splendor of the room. She surveyed the brown wicker furniture, smothered by overstuffed throw pillows, with approval.

The living room felt airy with its vaulted ceilings. The walls were painted a daring shade of ice cream-rich purple. Serena felt buoyed up by its soothing restfulness. Breathing deeply, as if hoping to taste the sweet smoothness by smelling, she realized she was inhaling a real fragrance. Tiptoeing across the plush ivory rug, she reached the gabled window's seat and the glass vase. Lilac blossoms plumed over the edge, and she couldn't resist sticking her nose into their coolness.

"Those are fresh from the back garden."

Serena lifted her head up. In her haste, her hair clip caught in the lace curtain. She worked at it gently with her fingertips as she looked behind her. A full-figured woman wearing a starched white apron hurried over.

"Let me help you, dear. It wouldn't do to snag that panel. Miss Emili just bought the furnishings for this room in Italy. She and Mr. Huff spent their entire anniversary month overseas— seeing as how it was their twentieth year of marriage. There you go, dear."

"Thank you."

"Oh, dear! Dan forgot a coaster again! How many times must I tell him to be careful not to get condensation on this sill?" She picked up the vase in one capable hand while she wiped the droplets with her apron. Without another word, she rushed out with it. She was back momentarily with a large wooden trivet. Once she had polished the window seat thoroughly, she dropped her apron and set the oversized coaster down.

Serena watched this lady, who appeared to be in her sixties, gently clink the vase onto it. She could tell that this woman never wasted a second of time. She stayed close to the wall, out of her way.

Unexpectedly, the woman turned, focusing her hazel eyes on her. "Serena, how are you? Miss Emili told me to expect you. I'm Barbara, the housekeeper. I've worked here for several years along with my husband Dan. The Huffs built us a small cottage last summer...back behind their flower gardens. It's the best place we've ever had. Mr. and Mrs. Huff have sure treated us good since hiring us on after my husband lost his hearing and his job. He fought in World War 2 in a tank. Back then, ear protection wasn't what it is now. Well, I have a 'to do' list a mile long."

Serena was thinking that Barbara must be older than she had thought when she caught a glimpse of two pairs of eyes peering at her from the hallway. She followed the housekeeper into the hall. Barbara patted their two heads as she hurried past them. "Good morning, Twins."

Serena tensed up. If she could help it, "the twins" would not come from her mouth. Those two words were endearing for **her** girls. Why was it that she must endure such poignant reminders when her grief was so fresh? She knelt in front of them. "Good morning, Girls. I'm Mrs...."

"Where's Mother?" one of the twins demanded.

The other one sulked as she twisted a small clump of hair around and around her index finger. Their mother had thought she should be absent for their first meeting. Serena was grateful to God for sparing her any chance of spilling unexpected tears that had a way of welling up at inopportune times. She felt like a crybaby clamoring for sympathy. She wished the cleansing tears would come at home, but they always tumbled down her cheeks in front of people. Even now she felt them stinging behind her eyelids and in her sinuses.

The girls' tousled hair reminded her of Brookelle and Joelle. When she brushed their hair, the natural curls glistened with a healthy shine. She could see why the housekeeper couldn't resist touching the disheveled silkiness. Leaning back on her heels, Serena gazed at the two look-alikes. "Your mother left for work, and I am here to watch you."

"No!" shouted one of the girls, jutting out her chin in defiance. She spun around and ran back upstairs. Her twin followed.

Serena exhaled slowly. She hadn't expected this though she should have been prepared, considering how hasty Allegra's emotions had been. Carl had always reminded her to think before she spoke. Looking at the schedule, Serena ascended after the petite four year olds. She needed to help them dress and fix their hair. A large family portrait hung on the wall at the head of the staircase. The girls did have eyes like their father's, but they resembled their mother in every other way.

"Girls," she called after them. "Please show me your room and your pretty clothes."

Barbara fixed their favorite breakfast of waffles and fried eggs. "Would you like a plate, too?"

Serena walked up close beside her at the stove. "It smells delicious, but no thank you. I've already eaten." Then in an undertone she said, "I learned the twins' names from the schedule, but the girls haven't cooperated to inform me which one is which. Will you kindly help me out?" She crossed her arms firmly across her stomach hoping to muffle the rumbling. Her own toast breakfast was hours past, but Miss Emili hadn't alluded that she could partake of meals. She would do nothing to jeopardize her testimony or position. She consoled herself that the sizzling eggs must be louder than her stomach.

"Blaire, I forgot to set out the forks. Will you please come and get them?" Barbara asked, glancing at Serena to see if she had caught the hint.

Serena rewarded her with a warm smile. Blaire was the one with the birthmark on her right cheek. She made a mental note that *Blaire* and *birthmark* both started with *b*. She glanced at the schedule once again. The meager lunch in her insulated bag would have to wait three hours to be eaten. Grateful for every hour not being planned out, she eagerly took them for a walk afterwards. Silently she admired Dan and Barbara's home. Window boxes decorated the front along with the lovely gardens.

Serena could have wandered in the balmy air much longer, but the girls were anxious to return to the house to watch a video. She managed to convince them to return outdoors with books. When she knelt with them beside the built-in bookcase in their bedroom, she became more engrossed in the titles than Claire and Blaire.

She knew how much Joelle and Brookelle would have enjoyed the large selection of books. On their way back outside, she retrieved her picnic quilt.

Serena encouraged them to snuggle, one on either side of her as she scooted back and leaned against the trunk of a maple tree. They sat stiffly beside her for a while as she read with expression about three helpful chicks. Gradually they began to warm to her, and Claire frequently interrupted to tell the story herself. Serena explained that it was difficult to have two storytellers. She began to take turns stroking the girls' hair while she read, and a gentle breeze that was scented with floral aromas toyed with the pages.

Serena yearned for the luxury of spending time with her sweet, innocent daughters. How she missed them being the ones to press against her arms, leaning in to see the pictures. They always preferred the wholesome books like she did…the ones filled with old-fashioned morals where family life was important. Fathers worked hard to provide and were a steady presence in the homes while mothers lovingly trained their children to enjoy doing chores alongside them, anticipating their return each evening. Even the illustrations portrayed tranquility and security.

With some effort, Serena had been able to persuade Claire and Blaire to look at some of their educational books. They seemed to appreciate the faddish women-in-charge characters. The modern "princess" types were bold and scantily clad. These four year old girls at her side were well on their way to becoming arrogant like their self-conceited examples. They hadn't been persuaded about the mystique of modesty and femininity.

Barbara came out with a tray of cups half filled with pink lemonade. Serena quickly finished the last two pages about shapes at a park as she approached.

"You need to follow your schedule better," Barbara advised, handing them each a clear plastic tumbler. The juice sloshed the ice cubes against the glossy sides.

"I'm sorry," Serena said. "We were engrossed in the books and completely lost track of time."

"You'll find out that Miss Emili and I won't put up with excuses like that. Disciplined schedules are important. This is the time youngsters should learn structured living."

Blaire gulped her last mouthful of lemonade then said in a sudden well-recited outburst, "Efficiency and sacrifice are what make life count." She set her empty cup on the tray with a flourish.

Barbara obviously satisfied the youngster's craving for praise by nodding her head vigorously. The youngster's smile was huge.

"If she doesn't already understand the key to productivity, I don't know who does," the meticulous woman said.

Serena felt dumbfounded as she stared at the schedule she had pulled back out of one of the books. She felt subdued as if all her initial efforts at winning the girls' confidence were in vain. The twins followed Barbara back to the house for flashcard hour. Serena followed with the books and blanket in confusion. She set the blanket in the car and looked at her watch.

She was only ten minutes late for drink break, and the girls had settled down and seemed to enjoy the books along with her. She didn't have an alarm on her watch, so from now on she'd have to be more in tune to what time it was. This was her first day, and they had been learning plenty from the books already.

When their mother returned that afternoon, both girls suddenly turned on accusing tears. Blaire lashed out angrily, "You didn't say goodbye in the morning!"

Mrs. Huff bent down and embraced them. "I'm sorry," she apologized.

The girls cried louder at her attempts to comfort them. Serena was shocked. Their behavior had straightened up for her. A haunting realization that Joelle and Brookelle were probably missing her emotionally distracted her from the scene before her. She focused on Dad and Mom's home in New York. What were her twins doing right now? Were they outside playing on the swing set? Would they be talking with each other about her and Carl? Maybe they were inside helping Mom cook supper with their little pink aprons and white chef hats on.

Serena's Mom had sent a picture of them baking brownies. Carl had been studying it one night where Serena had stuck it on the 'fridge. Tears quietly spilled from his eyes. Serena had wrapped her arms around his middle and rested her chin against his back. Then he sobbed, "It's all my fault."

Serena squeezed him gently but waited in silence. It wasn't often that Carl disclosed his innermost thoughts. She had only seen him cry twice...at Allegra's funeral and when they hugged the twins goodbye. "I never should have bought that older house. I should have known why no one else jumped at such a price. How I've learned the difference between cheap and inexpensive."

He paused to reach over the counter for a napkin. He loudly blew his nose and patted the moisture off his eyes and moustache. Serena went around and faced him while he continued, "Allegra would still be here if I hadn't bought that place. Why didn't I think about the stove being a threat? I wish I were a handyman like your dad." He stared at her with such wide, blank eyes that mirrored her grief.

"I'm just as much to blame," Serena argued. "I liked the house and was encouraging you to see its potential." But she could only think about the loud explosion as well. They'd have to wait until Heaven to see Allegra again, and they'd never get each passing day back with Joelle and Brookelle. She pressed against her husband, but Carl gently pushed her from him and went outside.

"Serena!" a lady's voice probed firmly into her reverie.

"Oh, yes," Serena said apologetically.

Miss Emili's brown eyes seemed large with questions, but all she said was, "You read outdoors?"

"Yes." Her mind scrambled for an appropriate explanation. Why did she sound so terse? The simple *yes* was still all her fogged mind could come up with.

Emili continued. "Around here we value our belongings and treat them with care."

"I under..."

"I'd appreciate it if you'd be an example to our girls of responsible frugality."

"We sat on a…"

Miss Emili slowly blinked and controlled the conversation.   Her lips seemed tight as she interrupted for the second time.   "I don't know what it is with you sitters. If only you knew how tiring it is for me to train each and every one of you."

Serena rushed over to the small shelving unit by the back door and grabbed her purse and keys.   "I'll see you tomorrow," she said as she hurried out the door.

Chapter Three

Adjusting

The warmth of the car's interior felt good. Serena hadn't realized how cold she had become while enduring the scolding. When she tried to steer her way toward the road, her hands were shaking.

She drove to a grocery store where food was the least expensive. It was then she discovered that her change holder was empty. She wouldn't be able to use a cart without a coin. "I even forgot the shopping bags," she groaned. "At least twenty dollars won't buy much."

She held her grocery list and slung her purse over her shoulder, bumping the car door shut with her hip. After following two heavy women into the store, she stood off to the side to evaluate which items should be priorities and to get her calculator. She caught a glimpse of dark pink in the bottom of her purse. Pulling it out, she started down the freshly washed tile.

A bag of flour was the first thing she balanced on her free arm. Funny looking numbers appeared on the little screen as she typed in the cost. Pressing the clear key, Serena pushed each number again. A jumble of broken lines showed for the second time. Then she remembered her scare the night before and how she had dropped her purse down the steps.

The calculator had been a gift from her father. Dad and Mom had home schooled her from sixth grade on. In fourth grade—attending a private school, her teacher had not managed time well. Serena only finished a third of a thick arithmetic book, and that teacher was asked to leave. She floundered through fifth grade despite Dad's teaching on her homework to clarify the different processes of converting and reducing fractions, about decimals, and the crucial foundations of pre-algebra.

They'd work into the late night hours at her desk trying to make up for all she had missed, but it was still slow going. Sometimes Mom would run to the twenty-four hour grocery and get a dozen doughnuts. It was her way of encouraging them since her three sisters would have already gone to bed.

Halfway through sixth grade as a home schooler and after much patient explaining on Dad's part, he finally broke through Serena's mind blocks. The mathematical formula he had learned from his algebra professor at the business school when he was a young man finally made sense to her. It was a simple concept of canceling that could be applied to many types of equations.

Serena gently returned the pink memento to her purse. She remembered how thrilled she had been when Dad's explanations had sunk in. No more gray areas but rather absolutes for the problems she had to solve. Then Dad had rewarded her with the calculator. Slinging the purse strap back over her shoulder, she proceeded down the aisle. She estimated high on everything, so she wouldn't cut herself short.

After arriving home, Serena selected the cold items and her purse and walked briskly through the long grass. Thankfully the door was already unlocked. Serena had parked behind Carl's truck, so she hurried upstairs knowing he was home.

Carl opened the second door. "What's wrong?" he asked immediately. His exceptional attention toward her and the concern in his voice stopped her short.

"Why do you ask?" she wondered.

"Because you're white, and your eyes look like a frightened deer's."

Serena set the groceries on the counter. "Oh, Carl, it's been one of those days. The calculator from my dad is broken. I smell like sour milk because the cashier accidentally spilled a gallon of milk, and it splashed all over me. Worst of all, I was reprimanded the first day on the job. There's still loose food in the car since I forgot bags. I'll be right back."

Carl firmly grasped her sleeve and said, "I'll get them." He brought in the last armful of individual things, and Serena eased the top layer out of his arms...the bagged rice, canned beans and cornmeal mix. He set the toilet paper and shampoo down as a package of disposable razors fell onto his black tennis shoes. "Tell me why on Earth you'd be scolded," Carl urged while he bent down to pick it up.

"I need to sit down and get my legs up, then I can tell you."

"Absolutely. Would you like some tea? I hope you don't mind, but I was so hungry that

I cooked up some boxed macaroni and cheese. I can dish up some of that for you as well."

"Thank you, Honey. Just tea for now. I'm too worked up to eat." She sat down in the semi-circle Japanese chair beside the thickly painted white, round table. They had found the four-chair dinette sitting on a curb with a bright orange free sign stapled to the table. It was unique, but hadn't been too difficult to clean up nicely.

Serena felt with her toes for another chair to rest her ankles and elevate her pulsating legs. How good it would feel to have Allegra rub at the itchiness and aching that felt like bruises. During the pregnancy for the twins, she'd been a terrific support to Serena. The second and third months brought all day "morning" sickness, so Allegra had cooperatively sat on the floor leaning against the couch while Serena rehearsed phonetic flashcards with her. Then Serena would read history and science aloud with her daughter snuggled beside her.

Allegra returned to the floor willingly when Serena asked, "Please will you massage my calves and ankles?" She'd read several books of her choice in payment before playing a math fact remembrance game. Once Serena reached the fourth month of the babies' gestation, she felt like a new person without feeling sick anymore. She and Allegra would try to be done with schoolwork promptly, so they could go for long walks together hoping they'd help her circulation.

Soon Carl was sliding a mug in front of her. The steam wafted away soothingly. He had left the almond and fruit tea bag steeping in the hot water the way she liked. He pulled out a chair and sat down quietly—waiting for Serena's account of her day. Serena reached across the table and squeezed his hand. "Thank you. It smells good. Remember when you and I used to explore our neighborhood on foot after we were married?"

Carl nodded. His eyes were sad. Their lives were void of pleasant times now.

After she recounted the entire day's happenings, she ended with, "Carl, I was completely unaware of the Huff's rule. I expected the girls to inform me...at least somewhat." She fingered some annoying tears away. "I'd never intentionally violate the family's guidelines, especially when I'm supposed to be an example to Claire and Blaire. From the bottom of my heart I want to be a Christian testimony to this family. This is my new mission field."

Carl watched her patiently while she paused to sip some tea.

Serena set her mug down and stared back at him affectionately. "Carl, you are such a good listener. You don't interrupt, and you have good eye contact which makes me feel like what I have to say is important to you."

"I've learned a lot from you and your family since we've been married," he responded humbly.

Serena smiled warmly. "Never before have I seen a mother cater to her little ones so. Honestly, she treated her children more like equals than myself. She made me feel like an immature dunce. The Scripture verse that says, 'Charity suffereth long...' keeps going through my mind. How I dread facing Miss Emili tomorrow.

"My calculator is broken, too. But wait...here I am rambling on and haven't asked about your day."

The phone rang shrilly. Serena jumped.

"I'll get it," Carl said, springing up. "Hello?"

Serena studied his face while she traced the mug's handle with her index finger.

"Hi, Honey," he said tenderly.

Knocking the chair over in her haste, Serena rushed to his side. Pressing close, she strained to hear their little girl's voice. Carl tilted the receiver between them.

"Grandma said she'll ask you; but, oh, Daddy, Brookelle and I really want to go!"

"Hi, Joelle," Serena spoke toward the phone.

"Mommy!"

That single word, uttered with such adoring passion, tugged at Serena's heartstrings until it seemed that the pain was unbearable. Looking up toward Carl, she could see that he missed the girls as much as life itself, too. Tears glistened on his moustache, and his lips quivered.

"Daddy! Mommy!" Brookelle squealed.

Both girls blurted out together, "Please may we go to Lancaster with Grandpa and Grandma?"

"We'll get to see a play!"

"And go shopping and eat at restaurants!" Joelle finished.

"Of course you may go," Serena managed to say for Carl who could only nod his head.

The twins responded with a delighted, "Yay!"

In a trembling voice, Carl said, "We love and miss you."

Serena's mom got on then. "How are you both doing?" Her tone was earnestly sympathetic which nearly caused Serena to sob aloud.

Swallowing hard, she replied, "We should be asking you that. We can't thank you and Dad enough for taking such good care of our girls. We're doing fine. I just started a job as nanny for twin girls. Please tell us, though. What's this about traveling to Lancaster?" She tossed her head to get her hair out of her face.

Carl fingered the individual cord spirals of the old phone they had purchased at the consignment shop that Serena had disinfected carefully.

"Well," Mom began, "the girls had their minds set on calling you last evening. After several attempts and no answer, they were devastated. I promised them that we'd try tonight, but I had to distract them in the meantime. Dad and I had already discussed taking them to the Christian theater, sightseeing and even spending one night in a hotel. We should have asked your permission first. I hope you don't mind."

"That will be good for them," Carl readily agreed. "I'll mail out a check as soon as I get this week's pay."

"No!" Mom was firm. "You put every cent toward your debts. We are just fine. Anyway, Joelle and Brookelle are our granddaughters. Dad is heartily agreeing. Just a minute...Oh, he said that he only wishes you two could go with us as well, at our expense. Anyway, don't think one more thing about it. Your girls are being so good, and we love having them. It's great to get to know them better."

After clearing his throat, Carl asked, "Which two evenings would be best for you if we were to call at set times each week?"

"Before I answer that question, allow me to clarify something. We will call you or else mail you a phone card. To answer you, I'd have to say that Tuesdays and Fridays would be best."

"That's perfect," Serena agreed.

"I'll put the twins back on. Take as long as you like. I'll say my 'goodbye' now. We love you both. Take care. Dad says that he's praying fervently for you each day as he drives to his work accounts."

"We love you and Dad, too. Thank you," Carl replied sincerely.

"How much longer until we can come home?" Brookelle wondered.

"We wish it could be tonight, Darlin'."

Serena added, "Daddy and Mommy are working very hard so that you girls will have a nice home. Right now we are in such a tiny place that we sleep in the living room."

Carl explained, "It's called a studio apartment, Girls."

"Brookelle and I could share a sleeping bag, so we wouldn't take up much space at all," Joelle pleaded.

Out of desperation, physically and emotionally, Serena collapsed onto the filthy rug and tugged on one of Carl's pant legs. She pointed at her outstretched legs. He hurried to kneel beside her with the phone. Serena rubbed at her knobby veins while Carl bravely tried to explain. "Girls, you need to concentrate on enjoying Grandpa and Grandma.   Think of this stay as a vacation. Mommy and I will be anticipating the phone call after you return from Pennsylvania. Did you know that Mommy and I also went to Lancaster?"

"You did?"

"Yes, on our honeymoon. Only we didn't get to see a play because the theater had recently burned like our house did. You'll get to see how God provided for it to be rebuilt. That will be an encouragement to you that God will do the same for us. He'll bring us through this valley."

"What's a *valley*, Daddy?"

"A *valley*, Joelle, is a low place between two mountains.   Spiritually, a valley can be a very difficult time that people go through.   We'll be waiting to hear you tell us all about the play, so watch and listen carefully."

"You were great on the phone with them." Serena kissed Carl firmly on his stubbled cheek. "I was remembering our honeymoon, too. Do you recall that afternoon you and I were walking across that huge parking lot?"

"The time you began twirling around?"

"Yes. It was out of character for me, but I wasn't embarrassed. I was—and am—so happy to be your wife. I felt free. All my dreams had come true by putting God first. I had my own secure, loving relationship that I had always seen Dad and Mom have."

All too soon the alarm was beeping. The bright red digital numbers blared 5:15. Serena hurried out of bed. She didn't intend to mar her reputation of being a little early—especially today. She was impatient with the dread and timidity she felt about facing Mrs. Huff. She plugged in the hair straightener before heading to the kitchen.

Preparing food first thing in the morning was a chore she disliked. Usually she tried to pack Carl's lunch at night, but last night she had washed her hair. Glumly, she opened a corner cupboard and grasped the peanut butter and honey. She set them down on the counter and stared for a moment at the cornmeal mix. Carl would much rather take Johnnycake than a peanut butter sandwich. Oh, well. She didn't have time to bake now.

She set the mix out as a reminder to make a double batch later. That way she could freeze a pan of it for next week. Time savers were becoming more necessary the longer she lived.

"What more can I do to save money?" she asked the butter knife as she held it up. A glob of peanut butter clung to the blade tenaciously.

"Exactly what I thought. No ideas. Your lips are sealed just like my mind feels. Carl trims my hair, and I shop frugally. I save presents that were given to me to use for others' wedding, birthday, or Christmas gifts."

She squirted the honey and spread it to the bread's edges. Carl didn't like dry crusts. "How much more is expected of me?" She stopped herself from flicking her wrist and tossing the piece of stainless steel into the sink. She gently set it down and took a deep breath.

"Instead I get blamed for being a typical young person who wants everything at once, like that lady at church said when we bought our house. Lord, please let her know somehow that we tried to buy within our price range and were living modestly..." her voice broke as she leaned her elbows on the counter and buried her face in her hands. She squeezed her cheeks, forcing herself to get going.

Grabbing for sandwich bags she had washed out the night before, she jammed in the sandwiches. Opening the 'fridge felt good as the cold air rushed over her. She bagged baby carrots, also, before punching everything into their insulated lunch sacks. Carl was usually up before

Serena, so she knew he must be tired. She returned to the bathroom, shutting the door quietly.

She resumed her prayer while she smoothed her hair with the heated iron. The heat only added to the mugginess. It was sticky already this early. She was determined to be well groomed despite being poor. If only the window in the tub surround would open. She'd tried several different times. It was sealed shut with layers of paint.

"Lord, You know my motives. I only encouraged Carl to buy our other home thinking it'd help us. We were barely paying more than the rent at our first apartment."

The hands on the clock opposite the sink read quarter to six. She set the straightener on the bamboo hot pad on the toilet lid before unplugging it. Her dark brown hair shone as silky as it could in the humid air. She had some natural wave that stubbornly frizzed out some. Serena ran the brush through her abundant hair and lightly froze it with spray. Then she began gathering the laundry to take out to the car.

When she arrived at the Huff home, Serena prayed. "Please set a watch upon my lips and guide me in all that I do today."

Mrs. Huff greeted her at the back door as if nothing had happened. "Good morning, Serena."

She even smiled brightly. Her white teeth shone clean, and her lips were smooth and healthy with a moderate application of clear lip-gloss. She wore a light pink blouse and pearlescent mint green jewelry. The colors seemed refreshing against her soft, olive skin. Serena found herself envying her healthy, moist complexion.

"Your instruction list is on the counter. I'll be returning late this evening. Please stay until my husband returns home since Barb isn't up to watching the girls."

Serena followed the list explicitly. She was polite to the girls, but she didn't try to warm to them after their betrayal. She dreaded meeting Mr. Huff all morning.

At lunchtime, Mrs. Kenaston surprised her and invited herself in. "I brought my lunch, but I thought I'd join you while you eat."

Oh, Mrs. Kenaston!" Serena enthused, rushing over from the kitchen table to give her a hug. "We were just picking up from their finger painting session. I'll wash their smocks and set the table."

The elderly woman sat down at the clean end of the table. She wasn't pretty; but she wore airy, cotton clothing that fit her well. Her hair was purplish white and was brushed smooth. Her discreet makeup of pinks and blues enhanced her fresh face. The way she folded her calloused hands in her lap and calmly waited seemed to invite conversation. She was a hard worker, yet Mrs. Kenaston never flaunted her ethics.

"Barb made lunches for the girls before she left for a doctor's appointment. My schedule says that they may eat outside at their plastic picnic table. Let me get them situated, and I'll be right back."

The girls set their cups down and scrambled onto the benches. Serena put their plates before them. Then she prayed to bless the food and hurried back inside. "Mrs. Kenaston, I've been wondering which house you work in."

"I work two houses farther up the road on this same side for Mr. and Mrs. Jasmine."

"What a lovely last name."

"Yes. Serena, how is the job working out for you? I've missed seeing you at the Laundromat lately."

Serena set her sandwich back down on the plate. "I'm still adjusting. I was scolded yesterday, and I'm not excited about meeting Mr. Huff later."

Mrs. Kenaston said, "I was afraid of that. I didn't want to scare you before the interview, but I owe it to you now. The Huffs can be cordial when they choose to be, and they'll never neglect paying you fairly. You must remember, though, that you are only responsible for doing your best. Beyond that, you answer to God and your husband alone."

Claire ran in with Blaire on her heels. "We want pudding."

Serena eyed the half-eaten bologna sandwiches on their plates. "You girls need to take three more bites first."

"No!" Claire stamped her foot while Blaire dropped her plate in defiance. Flavored tortilla chips smashed into pieces, spraying across the floor. The mayonnaise-covered bread and bologna landed wet sides down.

With effort, Serena said calmly, "Help me throw all this away."

Blaire ignored her, sulking. Claire looked directly at Serena but made no move to assist. Serena knelt down and smiled up at the double trouble. "Then no pudding for you." She picked up the rubbery bologna and wiped the linoleum with napkins. She located the trashcan in a nearby cupboard; but when she asked where the broom was, the twins remained quiet.

"Since you insist on being difficult, it will take me longer to clean up. So...we won't be taking a walk today." She began opening the largest, pantry-sized doors. Suddenly, little Joelle's and Brookelle's faces glowed vividly in her mind's eye. They were her double blessings. How she wished to feel their arms wrapped tightly around her.

Blaire stormed outside with Claire close behind.

"Oh, Serena!" Mrs. Kenaston exclaimed. "Someday God will reward you for your diligence of being faithful in that which is least and grant you a higher position."

Chapter Four

More Difficulties

Serena thought about those words all afternoon...when she played hopscotch with the girls and when she brushed out their hair. The Bible verse, "A word spoken in due season, how good is it!" was so true. Suddenly a chill ran tingling down her arms and nipped her fingertips. She had never thought to ask Mrs. Kenaston if she'd told Miss Emili that she had children. She hoped this job wasn't some sort of test regarding her character. She hadn't really meant to lie. She'd just skirted around the topic of children during the interview. Anyway, she'd make sure that she never missed work because of them. How could she anyway, being five hundred miles away?

Then she worried about Barb. It was nearly suppertime, and the chicken was defrosted on the counter. It didn't seem like her to shirk any of her duties. She hoped the woman wasn't seriously ill.

Serena had completed the list of activities with the children and had time to fill with them until Mr. Huff arrived. She thought of the picture in the upstairs hall. His penetrating gaze and rigid posture emanated the pride he felt in his family, yet somehow she sensed a subdued cheerfulness and humility about him. His left arm was wrapped around Miss Emili's waist possessively, and Claire was perched in a relaxed fashion on his left leg. Miss Emili held Blaire in her lap.

Serena sighed deeply and picked up the recipe for baked chicken and rice. She read it thoroughly before returning it to the counter. Barb had set out all the ingredients except the refrigerated ones. Serena decided to help her out. The directions were easy to follow. Allegra, Brookelle and Joelle had always begged to help her bake.

The thought caused her eyes to mist. She blinked fervently, calling to the girls. They ran into the kitchen. Eagerly they asked, "What are we going to make? May we lick the spoon?"

Serena smiled in spite of herself. Working side by side with her daughters had been part of her despite the extra messes and constant questions. "Do you girls ever help Barbara?" she wondered.

Blaire's wide eyes looked confused. "Barbara? No." Her response was solemn.

Claire, however, bounced on one foot then the other. "I want to help!"

"Yes," said Serena, "but first I need to know where the aprons are so that your clothes don't get stained."

Both girls looked at her blankly. Serena began her search in the spacious pantry. Not seeing any hanging up, she proceeded to look carefully through the drawers. Finally she peeked in the last cupboard. She hoped the girls noticed how she respected the belongings of their home.

She leaned against the countertop to think. "Perhaps we can clothespin bath towels around you," she thought aloud.

"What about our painting smocks?" Blaire suggested, skipping over to the sink where they hung secured to a white, plastic-coated metal rack.

"Excellent idea, Blaire!" Serena praised. She untied them and helped the girls into them.

She laid the cold chicken breasts in a thirteen by nine inch baking dish. Then she thoroughly washed her hands over one side of the deep, double sink. The girls took turns dumping the rice over the meat. Their arms constantly reached in front of her as they worked, slowing her down. Serena didn't mind. The knowledge that the love and joy she imparted as she taught them would remain with them as part of who they would become thrilled her soul. She thought that if they'd behave sweetly like this all the time, her career could be a pleasant one.

Serena scraped out the cans of creamy mushroom and celery soup over the rice and handed each girl a plastic spatula to smooth it. She poured in some milk before dotting the surface with butter. The girls rotated shaking the black pepper while she salted the food.

She lifted the glass pan and wiped it underneath with two paper towels before sliding it carefully into the preheated oven.

"Why did you do that?" Claire wondered.

"So no food from splashes on the counter will bake onto the oven racks or the bottom of the pan itself. It's much easier to prevent the mess than it is to scrub it off later." The heat wafted across Serena's face as she shut the oven door. After dampening a paper towel for each of them, she demonstrated--with the dishcloth—how to wash down the countertops. "We don't want to leave any bacteria, especially from the meat. Plus, leaving any food residue on kitchen surfaces can attract bugs and mice."

"Yuck!" exclaimed Blaire.

Serena nodded her head in agreement.

"What's *bacteriums*?" Claire asked softly.

"I'm glad you asked, Honey. After we wash up these few dishes, we'll look up *bacteria* in the dictionary." She was always amazed at how much easier she, as well as the children she was around, comprehended their textbooks' information after real-life learning. That's why she and Carl had always been on the lookout for interesting field trips. She made a mental note to ask if she would be permitted to take the girls on some educational outings.

The girls took turns washing and rinsing. Serena inspected each dish before drying it with the clean towel. Then they set the long dining room table properly. She explained to the children, "Be sure to set the forks on this side of the plates which is called the left." Stifling a yawn, she proceeded, "The knife blades must face the right sides, and the spoons go next to the knives." She followed after them, looking over their shoulders, rearranging the misplaced pieces.

"Hello?" a man's voice called from the side entrance.

"Daddy!" the girls cried out as he appeared from the hallway.

Serena held her breath and forced her lips into a polite smile. "Hello, Mr. Huff," she said.

"Yes, of course. A pleasure to meet you." He stretched out his hand.

Serena shook his hand before explaining, "Barb hasn't returned home yet, so the girls and I thought we'd fix supper."

"Thank you. It smells good. Dan, Barb's husband, had a nurse call me on my cell phone on the way home since he can't converse over the telephone due to his hearing condition. Barb's heart has been racing. The doctor wants her to be monitored at the hospital all night. She may need a pacemaker put in tomorrow. I suppose I'll head up to print ads off the computer for housekeepers until Emili gets home."

"Please, Mr. Huff, would you consider me for the job? I'd actually enjoy combining the two jobs. If it's all right with you, I'd like the chance to prove myself. Then if Barb feels well enough later on, she could assist me with easier tasks."

"Hmmm," Mr. Huff contemplated. "I'll give it some thought and discuss this with Emili later. It would be beneficial for the girls to learn how to clean. They need to be educated in all areas of life."

"The truck won't start," Carl informed her the next morning. "It's not the battery, and I don't have time to inspect it. You'll have to hurry because I need you to take me to work." He was quiet the entire way to the shop.

"It's a good thing we have two vehicles," Serena soothed as they waited at a light. She searched his face apprehensively. "I'll try my best not to keep you waiting tonight."

"No matter. If anything will go wrong, it'll happen to us." He continued to stare ahead at the traffic.

Serena cautiously steered the car down the unfamiliar driveway of Mrs. Kenaston's employ. The cool, foggy morning made her shiver. She was so uptight that she had forgotten to turn on the heater. She parked beside her friend's economy car and quietly shut her door. Before she reached the house, the door pushed out toward her, and Mrs. Kenaston held it wide. "What a pleasant surprise, 'Rena. I hope you'll have enough time for a warm orange cinnamon bun. Coffee's perking now. Come in!"

The kitchen was completely different from the Huffs'. It was boxier, and a homey fullness seemed to envelop her. She breathed deeply of the robust coffee aroma while taking in all of the polished wood. Every piece of furniture as well as the cupboards and flooring was glowing cherry and dark walnut. Porcelain plates delicately hand-painted in primary reds and yellows and rimmed in gold sat at an angle in a glass, wall-mounted buffet.

Then she saw the large clock. She had never been here, yet she was sure she had seen that exact clock before. The room's personality seemed uncannily familiar. It had an Old World feel. "Sit down, young lady." Mrs. Kenaston placed two saucers on the table. Delicate ribbons of steam escaped from the large iced buns. Serena's mouth watered. It seemed as if she could already taste the citrus tang along with the drizzled icing.

While Mrs. Kenaston poured the coffee, she asked, "What brought you here so bright and early?"

"Carl's truck isn't working. I took him to work this morning, but I was wondering if you'd mind picking me up for a few mornings until Carl gets it fixed. I'll pay you for gas, and I'll assist you with any chores you could use help with here before I walk over to the Huffs'. That way I won't worry about Carl waiting for me if I work late."

The elderly lady eased herself into the ornate chair opposite her. Serena contemplated the wealth contained in the kitchen alone. It baffled her as to how people could come up with the means to pay for college, medical school, nice cars and extravagant houses and still afford all the furniture and accessories. She couldn't even have an inexpensive new couch or table from a department store. If she and Carl were choking under the bondage of debt while living very frugally, how much more must the higher classes be silently strangling.

She didn't envy physicians' fast-paced, mundane lifestyle of work and little family time; yet here she was in the same situation without anything to show for it. Maybe it would be nicer to be a professional in some well-paying career. How refreshing it would be to return each evening to spotless home and tantalizing meals.

Mrs. Kenaston gently slid the sugar bowl and cream pitcher toward her.

"No, thank you. I usually drink my coffee black," Serena said. "Everything smells and looks delicious!"

"How was your first meeting with Mr. Huff?"

"It went well. He had some news to tell me which helped distract from the awkwardness. Barb is possibly in need of a pacemaker, and I might be filling in for her. Yesterday afternoon was wonderful because time sped by while the girls and I cooked supper. I feel like I'm home schooling again. The busyness helps distract me from salt being rubbed in my wounds, so to speak. Why couldn't the girls just be sisters? But no, they're twins that represent my own twosome that I long to be caring for."

With sincere empathy radiating from her tender eyes, her friend spoke, "My dear, I know from losing my husband that most people don't know how to 'weep with those that weep' as the good Book says. Always remember that I care. You are a partaker of Christ's sufferings, which is something you can rejoice about. Others may listen more attentively to you when they realize your life isn't perfect. I know this is a time of humbling for you. You see others whose lives always seem blessed and think you're being punished. That can be dangerous beginnings of selfishness and pride on your part. Anyway, gain doesn't mean godliness.

"Stay submitted to God, and I can promise you this...He will 'stablish, strengthen, and settle you.' He alone can make you perfect in Him and exalt you in due time. I've observed you trying to do that by continuing to let your spiritual light shine. Before I knew you, I saw you giving gospel tracts to people at the laundromat. Then when you sat beside me, you said, 'I asked Jesus into my heart as Saviour when I was four. Have you ever asked the Creator into your heart?'"

Serena swallowed her mouthful. "And you had that glow on your face. Your eyes answered the question for me before you said, 'I've also accepted Christ, Dear.'"

"Thank you, Serena, for being a humble, cheerful steward of the manifold grace of God even when you're broken inside." Mrs. Kenaston stopped to swallow hard. "Don't allow yourself to begin focusing your eyes on people. You know we'll always let you down. Only God can give you the ability to continue ministering." She dabbed at her eyes with a napkin.

The words, based on Scripture, rang true in Serena's heart. She sat still while they soaked in. A door shut upstairs, and she looked at her watch. "I have to go." She looked earnestly into her friend's green eyes. "Thank you...for everything." She grasped the last half of her roll and took it with her.

"I'll see you tomorrow morning," Mrs. Kenaston called after her.

The girls were already awake when she arrived five minutes early. "Serena!" they shouted, running into the kitchen.

Mrs. Huff followed them. A jealous gleam flashed across her dark eyes in an angry second. "Polite young ladies do not yell," she scolded. "Good morning, Serena. I must say that I was quite surprised with all that you accomplished yesterday. You seem more experienced with balancing children and housework than a young bride would." Her steady gaze seemed to be curiously re-evaluating her.

Serena felt squeamish inside. Forcing a smile, she answered, "I only hope I continue to please you."

Miss Emili breezed around the kitchen, the scent of her perfume wafting behind her. She opened up the refrigerator and set a salad into her lavender insulated lunch bag. "I'll continue to leave two separate lists. Do what you can on the housework and cooking. We'll see how well this arrangement works out." She added twisted cheddar and mozzarella cheese to the bag as well as croutons and a honey-flavored sesame seed bar then shut the door. "I figure that it's better to have more on the lists than not enough." She walked out of the kitchen and toward the side door. The girls followed her, so Serena did.

"Please be careful on the roads. The fog is thick today. I'll be praying for your safety."

Her employer stared at her for a moment before responding, "Oh, well, yes. Yes, of course. Goodbye."

Serena felt strange to have caught this assured woman off-guard. She had never seen her at a loss. After Mrs. Huff had closed the door behind her, Serena knelt down between Blaire and Claire. She talked aloud to the Lord. "Dear God, please keep the girls' mommy and daddy safe today while they travel. Lift the clouds from the roads so that they and other drivers may see clearly. Thank You for what You'll do. In Jesus' name, Amen."

Claire blurted, "Where are Daddy and Mommy traveling to? They didn't take suitcases." Her eyes were wide with concern.

"They didn't have sleeping bags either," Blaire said softly.

Laughter from deep inside rolled and heaved upward. Serena suppressed it to a chuckle. The joyous bubbling felt cleansing and freeing. The girls seemed more confused as they watched her with uncertain smiles. Serena held her chest, gasping for air. Finally, she was able to fill her lungs with a deep breath and explained, "*Travel* can mean journey, but it also means to go from one place to another. Your parents have left home to go to work."

"Oh," the girls responded together, obviously relieved. Then they each wanted to pray. Their tender, simple sentences were similar to her girls' childlike faith. The Bible even read something like that about a person needing to believe like a little child. *Suffer little children, and forbid them not, to come unto me: for of such is the kingdom of heaven.*

Chapter Five

Love of Music and Christian Family

Serena slid onto the organ bench before pulling out the pedal drawbar. On the floor beside the bench's other end, she wriggled her feet out of her dress shoes and slid them into her slippery flat shoes. Then she pulled the even-numbered drawbars.

The pastor's son, who was the main pianist, was looking at her. She smiled and nodded that she was ready. He began playing a faster hymn in his artful style. Serena didn't miss a beat. The full sound of the organ's harmonic richness colored in the threadbare spots of the familiar tune. Stephen demonstrated his enthusiasm by inserting runs.

Serena glanced at him across the platform as they neared the second verse. He mouthed silently, *You take the lead*.

She mouthed back, *Okay*. Unable to refrain a grin of pleasure, she took off—skillfully fingering the keys so the notes wouldn't sound detached. Stephen echoed her melody in chords. Serena saw the pastor climb the steps and walk toward his cloth-covered chair. The music director had paused in the center aisle to speak with a man. Nearly every pew was full. She finished the hymn's chorus before discreetly fading the volume with her left foot, pushing down the wide, ridged pedal. Stephen continued to play softly as Mr. Mattison approached the pulpit. "Good morning, folks! Please pick up a hymnal if you need one."

Serena flipped off the tremolo stop to give the organ its most majestic sound. It wouldn't clash with people's vibrato that way. The notes would have clarity. She rested her right hand's fingertips delicately on the surface of the Swell's keys. The accompanying fingers of her left hand found their places on the lower manual, the Great, again.

The organ was a moderate size with only two manuals (keyboards). However, the bass keyboard (pedals) that she played with her toes and heels intensified the richness of the tone. Her grandmother had taught her when she was aspiring to become the church organist at her parents' church at the age of seventeen. The pianist position had already been filled, and organists were hard to come by. Serena accepted the challenge of learning to become a good one. Grandma, an accomplished one herself, had explained, "Organ pedals have the same function as the bass. The bass would relate to the organ in the same manner the bassoons or tubas would to an orchestra."

Because of her thorough piano training, Serena was able to bypass much theory and had enjoyed developing organ technique. Stephen played an introduction with the hearty flourish of one who's mastered the principles and exercises. He evidenced confidence in every performance. Serena joined in whole-heartedly. She could feel the appropriate pedals through her thin-soled shoes as she slid them silently across the intervening keys.

The song director waved his hands in ¾ time. Down, up, in. Down, up, in. Down, up, in. The music flowed along a split second behind him as he led the congregation into the second verse. When they reached the chorus, Serena could no longer contain her joy. She sang an alto part while she played. She always told her piano students,

"Your diligence and patience throughout faithful practicing will bring rich rewards."

She knew it to be true. She felt rich while she accompanied Stephen.   When he had graduated from music school, he amazed the audience by playing a difficult piece with just his left hand.   As most pianists will agree, the left hand's fingers are the weakest. If the people had closed their eyes, they would have thought he was playing with both hands. Some parts demonstrated gusto while other movements displayed tender feeling.

He had invited her and Carl to his ceremony since he knew they'd appreciate hearing him. He seemed to draw emotion itself from the sounding board, and here she was praising the Lord along with such an accomplished pianist. Whenever time would permit, she yearned to resume her two hour rendezvous of scales, finger exercises and careful sight-reading. Then she'd practice playing by ear. Weren't there jobs anywhere that would allow her to practice eight hours a day as well as perform?

Mr. Mattison announced one more hymn. As the rustling pages grew quieter, Stephen started the intro.   Serena switched down an additional registration. The Diapason 8, Flutes 8 and 4, and Strings made a full sound along with the pedals on Bourdon 16.

For the offertory, Stephen played the primary part. Serena fingered a secondary melody counterpart, with no pedals, in a harp setting. Then, while she walked down to sit beside Carl, Pastor Eclant announced that there were young missionaries present. "Will you please come to the platform?"

Church members began gasping in surprise, exclaiming, "The Victors!" Serena felt her mouth drop open, but she was too numb to close it.

"Dominic and Merry came to see me at my office yesterday. They sought my blessing and counsel before announcing their calling publicly. Now I'll let Dominic tell you what has transpired in their lives."

Merry, who had been Serena's first Ohioan piano student, stood calmly beside her husband. Dominic spoke resolutely. "Brothers and Sisters in Christ, it is my privilege to inform you that God has called us to serve as missionaries in Sudan."

More gasps.

Dominic stared boldly at the crowd of one hundred fifty parishioners. "Believe me, I didn't even tell my bride about this until I had fasted and prayed, read my Bible for hours during the night, and prayed several more days. When I finally broached the subject, she said that she, too, had been exceptionally impressed about the dear

Africans. We know it won't be easy, but it's not easy for them either. I'd sure want someone to tell me how to be free from the guilt of my sins and how I could be guaranteed I'd arrive in Heaven someday.

"We'd be grateful if you'd earnestly remember us in prayer, and we'll be keeping you in our prayers." With that, he turned and gripped Pastor's hand before gently ushering Merry ahead of him down the steps.

Serena felt partly paralyzed. Pastor Eclant's message was droning in her ears. She turned to the text and tried to concentrate as her eyes followed along. After that, though, she could only think about the Victors. She had played the piano for their wedding two weeks before Allegra's death.

Pastor instructed the new missionaries to wait outside the auditorium after the invitation so people could shake their hands. Serena and Carl were toward the back of the line since she had to turn the organ off and straighten her music. The Pattons, a home educating family, were in line ahead of them. "See how God can use young people? Haven't I been telling you kids for years that Dominic had worthy goals and is a diligent worker?" Mr. Patton asked his four teenagers.

The boys and Suzanne grinned at their dad. Royce, the oldest, said, "As will we." Then he put his long arm around him, slapping his shoulder lovingly. Serena noticed that all the boys were taller than Mr. Patton. Suzanne was as beautiful as any seventeen-year-old girl could be, and she carried herself with as much poise.

Mrs. Patton's eyes twinkled at Serena. "It's thrilling to see results of home schooling. Merry and Dominic are starting out with a bang so soon after their support group graduation."

"That's for sure," Serena agreed. "Having finished Bible institute before his parents presented him with his high school diploma gave him a major head start."

Suzanne spoke up. "He schooled in the mornings, worked at the home improvement warehouse afternoons, and studied late after evening institute classes." Her earnest brown eyes were aglow with youthful vigor. Serena suspected this other previous student of hers had hoped to be in Merry's place. She was only three years younger than Dominic, and no one had suspected his attraction toward Merry until their wedding date was set. Dominic's mother had explained that he wanted the pursuit of her to be private and had courted her outside of church.

Serena felt for Suzanne. Young men with such ambition were few and far between these days. When they neared the young couple, an elderly veteran missionary was saying, "How wonderful to see you give up earthly fame and fortune to make a difference. Too many youngsters are seeking easy, noticed areas of service but missing what our lives are intended for. Don't let anyone discourage you about the dangers in Sudan. As you know, God is greatest of the mighty."

Serena watched as Suzanne politely congratulated Dominic and hugged Merry. The rest of the family followed suit. Then it was their turn. Carl spoke with Dominic while Serena hugged Merry tightly. Despite their age gap, Merry had been a true friend. With Serena's parents and sisters in New York, Merry had been like a sister to her. She'd occasionally help out with the children or housework and make life seem bearable while Carl was nearly always working. Merry spoke in her ear. "How are Joelle and Brookelle? Next time you talk with them, please tell them I said hello."

Mrs. Kenaston parked at the end of the Huffs' driveway. Serena ran out from the house and opened the passenger door. A balmy breeze whirled in around them as she shut it behind her.

"How would you like to eat out tonight?" Mrs. Kenaston asked.

"That sounds great!" Serena agreed.

Mrs. Kenaston sat quietly which caused her to look at the woman. Her eyes were fixed on Serena. She spoke earnestly, "As you know, I have no children. I married when I was middle-aged and miscarried two babies. How I mourned the fact that God chose not to bless my husband and me with little ones to cheer our home. Now that He's placed you in my life, I believe you have become like a real daughter. So as not to offend your mother by asking you to call me by a family title, would you please call me by my first name...Jerusha?"

Serena was overcome and could only think to say simply, "I'd be honored." It sounded so lame, but she was at a loss of expression. She wasn't a crier by nature, but many times lately her nerves felt so frayed that she felt like she were suppressing a swell of tidal sobs. Today, however, she just felt reserved and thoughtful.

Mrs. Kenaston's wrinkled hand pressed warmly on her back. Then she buckled her seat belt, and turned the ignition. She headed cautiously down the driveway and turned onto the road. "Carl is working tonight, right?"

"Yes. He's washing dishes at Lucinda's," she said.

"Would you like to eat there...or someplace else? My treat."

"I wouldn't mind eating at Lucinda's and seeing Carl bus some tables, but today isn't a good hair day for me. I wouldn't want to give the waitresses any more reasons to flirt with my husband."

"I understand," Mrs. Kenaston said, not taking her eyes off the pavement ahead. "Which sounds better...Chinese or Mexican?"

"Mexican food sounds good. Oh, Mrs. Kenaston...I mean, Jerusha! I haven't been to a restaurant in a long time. What a treat!" She took her eyes off the traffic on the highway and leaned her head against the cool window, looking up at the layered piles of fluffy clouds.

"We'll do Mexican then."

Before she pulled into the blacktop parking lot, they could smell meat cooking. The restaurant's waiting area was empty, and the hostess seated them promptly. Jerusha commented, "We timed this just right."

Shortly, a smiling Mexican waiter slid a plastic basket filled with tortilla chips onto the red table. Then he set two small yellow bowls brimming with juicy salsa beside the basket. "Welcome, Senoritas. Enjoy this tangy citrus-flavored salsa along with our homemade delicate corn crisps as a token of our hospitality. The cook will give your meals special attention now if you are ready to order." He grinned broadly once again, his white teeth brightening his handsome dark face.

Jerusha ordered a steak dinner, and Serena hesitated—waiting to see if he'd pull out a pen and order pad. He didn't, and his smile was expectant. She hastened, "I'll have the salad topped with refried beans and sour cream, please. Water to drink."

The young man walked briskly down the natural stone aisle then pushed one of the large wooden doors into the kitchen beyond. When the door shut, it completed a painting--along with the other door--of a sunny, Mexican countryside. Cultural guitar and mandolin music filled the otherwise deserted dining room with a subdued hominess.

"Serena," Jerusha scolded, "you should have ordered a heartier plate."

"I've been in the mood for a salad since I saw Miss Emili put one in her lunch a few days ago. Thank you, though. Perhaps I will add hot tea to the order later."

After she prayed aloud, Jerusha picked up a chip and scooped it into the freshly chopped tomatoes, green onions, garlic and dainty lime peelings. Specks of cut basil added color and aroma. Serena dunked a light chip into her bowl as well.

"Mmmm!"

Jerusha nodded in agreement as she finished chewing. After she swallowed, she said, "Mexican was an excellent choice! This fresh salsa does hit the spot." She selected another chip before looking directly at Serena. "I sense that you haven't had a good talk in a while. Please tell me more about your life before Allegra's accident."

"We had bought an old house since it'd be comparable to renting, and we'd gain equity. I was willing to work with a cosmetically challenged home and fix it up economically over time. All summer I gladly washed dishes out in the yard with the garden hose until we could afford plumbing renovations. However, one major thing after another went—despite the three hour home inspection before we bought it. Carl had followed the inspector around for two of those hours since he couldn't get off work sooner.

"Carl thought that he was thorough, but even an inspector can't guarantee anything. The hot water heater needed to be replaced. Then the well pump died. There was no well cap, so the ground had to be dug up which led to the discovery that the lining was bad, too. In late summer, we called a reputable plumber to clean the furnace in preparation for winter. He told us that the furnace was old enough he wouldn't be able to find a part it needed. He said we could try to limp it along and see if it could function but warned us that it might quit...and who's to say that it wouldn't do so on the coldest day of winter?"

"Oh, Serena!" Jerusha moaned sympathetically.

"Carl dutifully buckled down to meet his responsibilities. He's worked two full-time jobs back to back. He worked third shift at a warehouse loading tractor-trailers, left there at six thirty a.m. to drive straight to his machining job until the warehouse shut down. That all night shift was the most wearing on our marriage. We were leading completely different lives. I had to keep the children quiet all evening."

The waiter approached them with a full tray. "The cook was fast," Jerusha noted. "May we please have some hot water for tea?"

Serena observed that the orders were filled correctly as he set their plates in front of each of them. She hurried to eat a chip so he'd see that she wasn't through with her appetizer.

"I've kept you talking, and you haven't been able to eat. I want to hear the rest of your story later if you don't mind."

They were silent as they worked on the food. A large party was ushered in and seated across the room. The young man returned with the hot water and tea bags. Serena sipped the piping hot drink gingerly as comforting steam bathed her face. She watched the Mexican scurry around the newcomers' tables that the hostess had shoved together.

"Jerusha, that man doesn't write anyone's order down. How on Earth does he remember every detail such as who asked for creamer or which salad dressing and all the rest?"

Jerusha stopped cutting her tender steak to watch. "That's a good question all right."

Serena had eaten three fourths of her salad, and Jerusha's steak was gone when he carried out the first tray. A bus boy followed close behind with another. The waiter efficiently distributed all the salad and the various dressings while instructing his assistant regarding the drinks. No one seemed to question what they were given. The two returned shortly with main courses and repeated their performance.

Serena and Jerusha stared at each other incredulously. Jerusha's eyebrows were raised question marks. "We can't disbelieve what we just witnessed, but I surmise he must have a recorder hidden on his person or a photographic memory. He deserves a good tip."

Serena discreetly looked in her wallet. Since Jerusha was paying for the meal, the least she could do would be to pay the tip. All she had was a twenty-dollar bill that she had saved for the laundromat.

Jerusha left a tract on the table with several bills sticking out as they left. She commented on the sombrero wall hangings. "Something like that would look good in my kitchen."

"Thank you for the delicious meal, Mrs. Ken-...I mean, Jerusha."

"Will all these steps be okay for you...Jerusha?"

Jerusha walked with Serena toward her apartment since Carl wasn't home yet. "I still carry the vacuum cleaner up and down two flights at Bethany's, and I'm eager to see pictures of your family."

"I baked sugar cookies last night. Are you ready for dessert and coffee?"

When they were both seated at the table, Serena suddenly put two and two together. In her mind's eye she could see the familiar clock in the kitchen at the home of Jerusha's employer. Its hand-painting of a pastoral countryside on the rich wood above the face was identical to the scene she remembered seeing at her friend's as a teenager...Bethany's home. She lived in New York as well. Could it really be that they had both settled in the Dayton area?

After a Wednesday night church service, Suzanne Patton approached Serena as she was straightening up the music rack on the piano. She had filled in for Stephen who was out of town for a piano competition. Carl, who was waiting nearby, informed Serena that he needed to talk with someone and would meet her at the car.

Suzanne asked, "May I speak with you, Mrs. Callahan?"

"Sure." Serena slid off the piano bench and led her to sit down beside her in the auditorium.

Awkwardly, Suzanne struggled to begin; so Serena quietly suggested, "It's not easy waiting for the right young man is it?"

The young lady seemed relieved and looked up in surprise. "How did you know?"

"I was a teenager once, you know; and I suspect that you were attracted to Dominic Victor. Am I right?"

The girl quickly looked down. "Was it that obvious?"

Serena was reassuring. "Suzanne, you have been a terrific role model for other girls by your modesty and guarded attentions. I picked up on the respect you displayed for Merry's new husband by the way you praised his character traits. I admire your taste for Godliness and hard work in a man. He's good looking, too; but I believe you were drawn to his personality."

Grateful for someone that understood, Suzanne opened up. "I should have guarded my emotions better, but somehow I was always attracted to him. Another young man has been asking my dad about me, but I've asked him to stall for me. I had always hoped Dominic would notice me someday and that I'd be good enough for him. I prayed a lot for him, too."

Serena sat silent for a moment, hoping her eyes portrayed her compassion. "Suzanne, my grandma once told me that there are more fish in the pond. I wasn't thrilled to hear it then; but over time, I began to see God's hand in my life. As much as I had admired a young man in my church, I knew that it would be wrong on my part to pursue or force myself upon him...just like you. Actually, I had never noticed him before until his mom began asking for prayer for him. His dad had recently died, and he was leaving for college to prepare for medical school.

"I started to observe him when he was in town only because I was somewhat aware of his situation because of his mom. His initiative and personality...and looks...were hard to beat. ~I feel for you, Suzanne.~ Somehow his mom picked up on the fact that I liked him. She must have mentioned it to him, because she carefully told my mom that he thought he'd be robbing the cradle to marry me since there was a six-year age gap between us. I wondered why he cared so much since he still had all of college and medical school to go through. Couldn't he at least get to know me? The worst thing that could happen, I thought, is that he could give me a ring; and we'd wait to marry until I was older.

"I ached inside and shed many secret tears over him. I was mortified to think that he may be thinking of me as a flirt but held onto the hope that someday I'd have the chance to prove to him that I was mature enough and that I'd make him a good wife. That never happened, so I went on trying to prove my worth to myself by working hard. My mom and sisters always wondered why I was so impatient to be married at such a young age and probably thought I was ridiculous to set such high goals for myself rather than enjoying life as it came. I would have been fine if I hadn't ever heard about him in the first place. Sometimes I mourned the day that I first heard his name."

Suzanne nodded, her moist eyes eager, as she asked, "So how did you get over him, Mrs. Callahan?"

"It wasn't easy, Suzanne. I read my Bible, prayed and practiced the piano a lot. I did more than my share of chores around the house...anything that I could do to keep myself preoccupied. I carried index cards around with memory verses written on them. Then the summer I was eighteen, a young man that moved into the area began attending our church. I didn't pay him much mind because I was still struggling, and I knew that my younger sister was the real beauty in our family. Most people thought she was several years older than I and were attracted to her outgoing personality."

"It was Mr. Callahan, right?" Suzanne guessed.

"It was." Serena smiled, squeezing Suzanne's hand in a sisterly gesture. "When he asked my dad about me, I was shocked. Could anyone really like me? Dad reminded me that God had heard all of my prayers and knew just the man I needed. Then he proceeded to tell me that he was very impressed with Carl's sincerity and that he always had foreboding concerns about the other young man. I trusted my father's judgment implicitly although I didn't love Carl at first sight.

Our love had to grow over time. Now I see, over and over, Dad's wisdom and God's protection.

"The man I believed I had really loved, rather than just being infatuated with, went on to marry a girl younger than myself after I married Carl. He probably makes her a loving, good provider. However, I count myself blessed because I have a husband that has allowed me to home school even when it's been tough financially. Now that I've had years to mature more, I can see my dad's concerns. He may be the type that would say, 'Send the kids to public school and get yourself a job.' Instead, I have a husband that believes exactly the way I do...to value our children as our most precious possessions.

"He told me a while ago that he couldn't bear to see our girls boarding a bus, knowing that they'd be in danger of knife wounds or being shot. How could we send them to a school where God is ridiculed? How can anyone have a better god than one that died for him or her? All these false religions promote being good enough to please their gods or even self-destruction, and justify forcing others to accept them or killing them."

"You have helped me so much, Miss Serena," Suzanne thanked her. "Will you pray with me before we leave?"

"Of course I will, Suzanne. Dear Lord," Serena began gently, "please help Suzanne to rest completely in You. Perhaps the young man that's been asking about her...needs her personality, her confidence in her God-given strengths, and her energies. You made her to be a helpmeet to one man. Maybe he isn't exactly what she thinks she needs, and maybe he isn't. I just pray that she won't dismiss him too quickly until You give her and her parents peace one way or the other.

"I always like the verse in Proverbs that says, 'A virtuous woman is a crown to her husband.' It may be that because of her faithfulness and support, her husband will be known in the gates. We thank You for the verse in Proverbs chapter thirty-one where it says, 'Strength and honour are her clothing; and she shall rejoice in time to come.'"

Suzanne gave her a hug and promised that she'd keep her updated. Then she left. Serena followed behind, suddenly feeling heavy hearted as she remembered once again that she needed to be completely honest with Mr. and Mrs. Huff. She determined to explain first thing in the morning that she was experienced with children.

Chapter Six

Mystery Resolved

"**M**iss Emili, may I speak to you before you leave please?"

Emili paused to look at her. "Of course."

Serena felt her face growing warm while her hands felt cold. Determined to have the dreaded confession over with, she plunged right in. "Miss Emili, I need to apologize for keeping the whole truth from you about my family situation. I didn't want to disqualify myself before you'd even consider me since I knew that I'd care for your girls like my own." A frog seemed to clog her voice. Emili's eyebrows arched at the last three words.   She crossed her arms but remained silent.

In embarrassed frustration, she cleared her throat and opened her eyes wide to stare at the light momentarily. She didn't intend to come across as a sympathy seeker...especially to this woman. She continued, "Carl and I were already living as frugally as possible when we had a gas explosion that engulfed half of our home and killed our eight year old daughter. We had no way to make ends meet—especially since our insurance lapsed. My parents took our six-year-old twin girls to live with them in New York. I was desperate for this job so that we may reunite our family as soon as possible. I had home schooled them and poured my all into them just like I'm caring for your girls. My mom takes excellent care of Joelle and Brookelle, and I don't foresee any problems that would interrupt my responsibilities here."

"I wondered," Miss Emili said. "You seem way more comfortable with children than I expected."

Serena's heart began to race. "I realize that I betrayed your confidence and understand if you need to let me go." She held her breath as she waited for her employer's answer.

"You poor dear!" Miss Emili responded. "Despite your grieving, you've treated the girls wonderfully. And you have twins as well. It must be difficult working with others when you miss your own."

Serena was astounded by her reply. "Well, I've been concerned that, for some unexpected reason, someone might call for me...only if it were an emergency, of course. I'm a Christian, so I need to live like Christ in every area of my life."

Emili turned abruptly. "I appreciate your getting things out in the open. I need to leave momentarily. Thank you, Serena," she said with an air of professionalism.

"I appreciate your time, Miss Emili," Serena called after her.

Mr. Huff came home early that evening, and Barb had been gradually taking back over her responsibilities. Barb would say, "I don't know how you cleaned the house, cooked, and schooled the girls. Then again, you're young and can handle it. I'm grateful to you for saving my position for me."

"I enjoyed it, Barb. Please allow me to take you grocery shopping Saturday after I work my half day." Barb agreed, and Serena gathered her things to walk toward Jerusha's house of employ. She wondered if she would still have a job in the morning. Miss Emili was always a stranger somehow. One moment she would actually be friendly until some internal switch suddenly transformed her into a rude authoritarian.

"Lord," Serena prayed aloud, "thank You for what You will do. I've bathed this situation in prayer. Please help me to have peace in my heart or guide me to another job."

The vehicle situation was still not resolved. Serena paid Jerusha gas money each week, but she longed not to be dependent on her friend. She reached the end of the Huffs' long driveway. She crossed the street to be on the left side. She walked briskly as she thought more about the truck. Carl had asked a friend from work to look at it. The man hadn't been encouraging about all that it needed. Since then, the car had also developed a problem that Carl tried to repair by using permanent bonding automotive glue. He limped it to both jobs and home again.

Serena felt much safer riding with Jerusha, and she tried to compensate her for the inconvenience by inviting her to eat supper at the apartment sometimes and putting quarters in the washers for her when they went to the laundromat together.

The warm summer air began to revitalize her. Everything would be all right. She was God's child. She pulled out an index card from her pocket with a memory verse written on it in her neatest script. "Job 12:10—'In whose hand is the soul of every living thing, and the breath of all mankind,'" she recited aloud to herself.

She was nearing the driveway when she heard someone slowing down behind her. Then the same red sports utility vehicle that she had passed the day she was hired turned onto it. Serena's heart skipped a beat. Could it really be Bethany? Feeling awkward to follow the car, she hesitated on her side of the street. Once the vehicle was out of sight, she crossed the street and walked slowly down the recently sealed drive.

She couldn't stop creating scenarios in her mind. Maybe she'd actually get to speak with Bethany. What if she wasn't cordial to the lower class anymore? Serena decided that she'd just wait in Jerusha's car. When she reached it, the doors were locked. Leaning against the passenger door, she pondered what to do. Jerusha should be out soon. Usually she finished her work first and drove over for her. The house door opened and shut. Serena looked over her shoulder and saw that it wasn't Jerusha. It was…could it really be Bethany? She wouldn't be expecting her. Not wanting to startle her friend, she figured it'd be better to call out rather than waiting till she was startled by her presence.

Before she could, her home school friend of years past was looking straight at her and running, her heels clicking. Then she stood before her as they stared at each other for one disbelieving moment. Bethany fit the part of a wealthy doctor and doctor's wife. She wore a long linen jacket over a silky lavender shell and dark skirt. Her modern square-toed shoes were cream colored to match her sport coat. Her hair was as dark as ever. "Serena!" the familiar voice finally said.

"Bethany" Serena answered but waited to move out of respect.

Suddenly Bethany embraced her, and Serena hugged her back tightly. Both of them squealed softly in delight. Then Bethany grasped Serena's hands. "Please come in," she urged, leading her. She ushered her into the elegant living room and called out to Jerusha, "Mrs. Kenaston, please bring some iced tea."

There was more organized clutter than the Huffs' had, but it lent hominess like a full restaurant with lots to look at. A fireplace on a raised hearth with a black screen and wide marble seat attached to its front reminded Serena of Bethany's childhood home. They had sat on the warm seat often to talk.

Bethany pulled Serena toward it in her outgoing manner. "As you remember, the hearth is warm in winter and cool in the summer." It was reassuring to see her so unchanged. Then she slid onto the thick slab of marble and amiably patted the surface beside her.

Serena obliged with a broad smile. "How did you know that I was loitering in your driveway?"

Bethany laughed her feminine-sounding, carefree lilt. "When I passed you out on the road, I didn't recognize you as a neighbor that usually walks. I mentioned to Mrs. Kenaston that we possibly had a new neighbor. Then she spotted you through the window. She perked up and asked me if you were the one."

Jerusha bustled in carrying a tray laden with coffee cups and a matching carafe. A variety of small, delicate pastries dusted with confectioner's sugar adorned one of the hand-painted plates Serena had noticed before in the kitchen. She set the tray on a glass-topped bamboo cart that Bethany had pulled in front of the hearth seat. Jerusha said, "As soon as I said that we were friends and told her your name, Miss Bethany went racing outside. May I ask how you know each other?"

"We became friends through our home school support group in New York State where families meet once a week or so for sports or drama along with other classes that parents with different strengths teach to groups of children," Bethany explained.

"Yes. Even though I'm two years older, that didn't matter. That's a very nice benefit of being schooled at home," Serena added. "We generally relate well to all ages."

"I believe that," Jerusha agreed with merriment in her eyes. " Just fancy the two of you moving and settling in the same area when you have the entire United States to choose from." Looking at Serena, she said, "Don't rush. I can always find things to keep me busy."

Chapter Seven

Face to Face

Serena was sitting on the library couch with the girls snuggled beside her one afternoon when she heard the doorbell. Barb wasn't there, so Serena knew it was up to her to answer. She expected to see Jerusha but was surprised to see Bethany standing on the front step. "Hello, Bethany!" Serena greeted her warmly. Her friend's dark hair was pulled back softly into a feminine twist though some curled around her face in shiny wisps. Her long coat was tailored to her slim body. She didn't wear much jewelry, but her gold hoop earrings and sparkling diamond were enough. Bethany had never liked dazzling beauties but preferred those who tastefully wore genuine adornments...another way her childhood culture emanated itself.

"Is there a place we can talk in private?"

"Well, uh, yes," Serena said uncertainly.

"Come on into the parlor." She hoped Miss Emili wouldn't mind her entertaining in her home. She had never thought to ask about such a situation, and her employer had never specified. Hopefully Bethany would be quick and take her leave before either of the Huffs returned. Her eyes seemed to take everything in as Serena walked beside her.

Once they were seated on the wicker furniture, Bethany said, "I was hoping you'd play the piano for my party this Friday evening."

The house was silent as she waited for a response. When Serena recovered from the surprise, she began, "You won't have..."

"Of course I won't have alcoholic beverages. What do you take me for?" Bethany interrupted. "Will you do it for your old friend? Say you will, 'Rena. It'll just be an early Christmas get-together for doctor friends of ours since the Christmas season is too busy, and I'll be the envy of all to have you playing in the background."

"I'll need to practice. Do you have a list of songs you'd like me to play?"

"No. Just traditional songs suitable for the season. I trust your judgment. Plan on being at my house by seven o'clock. The party won't begin until eight. Will that give you enough time to arrange your music and familiarize yourself with my baby grand?"

"I should be fine with that if I'm able to practice on someone else's piano before then; but if not, may I arrive at six?"

"Absolutely. Just give me a call. Here's my business card. My home phone is the last one listed." She stood. "If you will excuse me, I'll get on home. I stopped here on my way back from the office. I had been wondering what to do differently for this year's event. I don't know why I didn't think of you sooner. The invitations specified black ties and formals, so your playing will set the mood. I am grateful to you for helping me at the last minute like this."

"Thank you for asking. I'll walk you to the door."

Bethany complained as they walked. "My husband is never any help with these occasions. He won't give me any suggestions or mingle well during my parties. I don't know why I married an older man. I should have known he'd be no fun. He always says that he'd rather spend time with me and adopt a child. I don't have time or the energy to have a baby, " she sighed disgustedly. Shaking her head, she said, "Really, I'm not the homebody, nurturing type of person."

Serena didn't know what to say. She knew that was true about Bethany. She liked to be loved but didn't know how to return it. How Serena craved time like that with her husband and daughters. "I'll be praying for you," she managed to say.

The twins had been waiting in the hall and gazed curiously at Bethany as the women left the parlor. Serena heard Emili's voice as they made their way toward the door. She tensed up inside and hastened her steps. Bethany didn't rush but walked sedately behind her. Claire and Blaire called to their mother, "We're near the parlor, Mother!" Serena looked behind her apprehensively. To her chagrin, Miss Emili was walking toward them.

"I thought I recognized Bethany's vehicle in the driveway."

Bethany came around Serena and explained, "Good afternoon, Emili. We're always long lost neighbors in the winter." She laughed lightly. "Serena and I have known each other since we were teenagers in New York. I came to request Serena's help with a colleagues' party. I intend to have a neighborhood party sometime after the first of the year. You'll be invited. You have a lovely home."

"Thank you," Miss Emili responded. "Are you and your husband doing well?"

"We're fine," Bethany stated simply. "The people profession always keeps us busy. No day is the same. We both have as many patients as we can handle."

"I can relate," Emili agreed. "Won't you have a smoothie with us?"

"Thank you, but, no. I haven't been home yet. I left work early to finish my preparations. My husband won't be able to eat without me, so I need to get busy. Sometimes he smothers me with his politeness. Goodbye."

"Farewell," Miss Emili said.

"Goodbye," Serena called quietly from behind.

Serena worked harder than ever the following day. Finally, an hour before Emili was expected to return, Serena checked the last chore off the list and settled the girls beside the piano with books. Sitting down on the bench, she fingered the keys lovingly before she began to play some Christmas songs from memory. Each one led into another, and she was soon oblivious to her surroundings. A beautiful world of possibilities opened up around her. She imagined that she had mailed an application to the Grand Pianoforte Conservatory Contest in New York City, that Stephen had told her about, and was accepted.

Then she played "What Child Is This?" Her

mind played tricks on her, and Claire's and Blaire's reflections in the piano's gloss behind the keys changed into Joelle's and Brookelle's. They smiled at her and held up their dolls. She modulated into "Lo, How a Rose E'er Blooming" and glided through the syncopation with ease. The plaintive Old German melody resounded with the emotion she urged into the keys. Suddenly Emili was there beside her. Serena stopped abruptly and looked up.

"First, you entertain in my home. Then the very next day, you ignore the girls and play the piano."

Serena opened her mouth to explain that she had completed all the girls' preschool assignments as well as the chores, but Miss Emili didn't allow her a second. While she continued to scold, Claire interrupted to show her mother the mosaic craft they had made earlier out of uncooked noodles and pretzel sticks. Serena hurried downstairs and left.

She spent a normal lonely evening at home while Carl was at the restaurant. She ate a quiet supper of scrambled eggs and buttered toast. Then she settled on the couch and placed her mug of tea on the end table so that she could rest her Bible in her lap. She was reading through Ezekiel in her devotions and had already read a chapter that morning. Instead of resuming there and getting bogged down in all the temple measurements, she flipped through the thin pages. She scanned over the individual verses and passages she had underlined in the past.

She read how Jesus didn't speak a word to his accusers. Coming upon James 3:2, she read it over and over. "For in many things we offend all. If any man offend not in word, the same is a perfect man, and able also to bridle the whole body."

Serena forced a nervous smile when Mrs. Huff greeted her the next morning. She was as mysterious as ever. No apology or smile, but no anger either. She just went on as if nothing had happened. Serena hoped it would be better that way though she wasn't accustomed to brushing things under the rug. She had been taught, while growing up in her Christian family, that no one should let the sun go down upon their wrath. They should work out any disagreements.

As Miss Emili discussed the day's events hurriedly, Serena waited for an opportunity to apologize again. However, the woman never paused. Two of Serena's memory verses came to mind. *He that hath knowledge spareth his words:*

and a man of understanding is of an excellent spirit. Even a fool, when he holdeth his peace, is counted wise: and he that shutteth his lips is esteemed a man of understanding. She bit her tongue and listened.

"I saw your written comment in the girls' school log yesterday. That would be fine if you'd like to take them on a field trip to learn more about the Wright brothers. Just be back by suppertime." She buttoned her dressy full-length leather coat and walked down the hall toward the door.

Serena watched her sporty vehicle go down the driveway through the sheer curtains. It was a struggle not to feel animosity in her heart. She forced herself to quote the verses in Daniel that she had memorized the night before. Chapter one verses three and four spoke of Daniel and other Israeli children who were well favored and skillful in knowledge. She prayed quietly, "Please, God, may I purpose in my heart to glorify You."

Verse nine had seemed to jump off the page last night. "Now God had brought Daniel into favour…with the prince…" She said the words out loud, "Now *God…*" She turned from the window to go wake Blaire and Claire. If only she could come to grips with the fact that the God the entire universe loved *her*, and He would steer her life—and Carl's—in the right direction. It wasn't so much that He *would* that she struggled with but that He *was* guiding them—here and now. It didn't take Him by surprise that she was separated from her own flesh and blood and caring for others. So why was He allowing it?

Even as she thought it, she was convicted. Wasn't that the same sacrifice Jesus had made? He came from Heaven to be a man of sorrows Who was acquainted with grief much more than she. He even had a humble carpenter job. He knew what it was like to be despised and rejected.

Serena yanked a tissue from a nearby box. She dabbed at her eyes then went to the kitchen to throw it away. As she pushed in the lid, she gasped. The girls' older porcelain dolls were laying forlornly on top of the other trash. She nonchalantly verified with the girls that they were indeed supposed to be discarded. "Yes," they assured her heartily. "We don't like them anymore since Daddy bought us new ones. Mommy said that we had to throw them away."

When they went upstairs to get dressed, Serena quickly rescued the neglected beauties and replaced the bag, tying up the full one. Quietly opening the back door, she hurried outside. She placed the dolls gently under her seat in the car before dropping the garbage bag in the outside can. She had returned to the kitchen by the time Blaire and Claire came down for breakfast.

Chapter Eight

Sticking by the Stuff

Serena was quiet on the way home. Jerusha gently probed, "Is everything all right, 'Rena?"

Serena glanced at her elderly second mother in the car's dark interior then watched the path the headlights made on the expressway. "I'm fine. It's just been an emotionally exhausting day. Barb offered me her car, so I could take the girls to the Wright brothers' museum in Dayton. I hit a nail on the way home. We were stranded by the side of the road, and I had forgotten to borrow Carl's cell phone for the day. I couldn't let the Huffs know or call the police for help without getting out and walking, and it wasn't a safe part of town.

"We locked our doors and prayed for a police

officer to come by. One did, but he didn't stop. I flashed my lights hoping he'd see in his rear view mirror despite the sunshine. I saw his backlights come on and back off again, so I hoped he meant help was on the way. We were beside a stoplight; so every time it turned red, the other drivers were staring us at. Talk about feeling defenseless. Finally a policeman did come and kindly changed the tire for me to get home.

"Miss Emili wasn't too happy with me by the time we got back. She was worried sick that I had kidnapped her girls. One good thing that came out of it was that I got to see that Barb and her husband Dan sure trust me now. They stood by me and backed me up until Miss Emili calmed down, and the girls explained how God had answered our prayers while we were waiting."

Jerusha nodded.

"And another thing. Whenever I see Bethany while I'm waiting for you, she chatters about surface stuff like I'm a mere acquaintance or complains about her husband. She asked for my phone number, but she hasn't called me once. Jerusha, I thought of her as one of my closest friends. What makes people that have so much in common change and part ways?"

Jerusha was quiet for what seemed like a long minute. "It's choices, honey. Ultimately people choose the directions they go, by their daily priorities."

"I guess that's what bothers me. I want to be sure my friends aren't choosing different friends because they think I have misplaced values?"

Jerusha glanced at her with silent questions in her wide eyes.

Serena weighed her thoughts before speaking slowly. "For instance, my friend at church is now a missionary. She doesn't have time anymore to talk briefly at church. People surround her and her husband the moment a service ends with questions to ask and well wishes to offer. I'm glad for Dominic and Merry, and I realize that I'm just experiencing withdrawal which must come sooner or later. After all, she'll be living in Africa when their deputation is finished. I can only imagine what their schedule is like being gone nearly all the time visiting churches to present their ministry and only home occasionally."

"Don't you have others that you can talk with at church?"

"Yes," Serena answered. "I have former piano students and their parents and other pleasant acquaintances, but none of them inquire as much into our personal lives. Merry was like one of my sisters. Sometimes she'd come and watch the children for me so that I could use her car and go shopping or else assist me with housework. There were times that we'd put the girls to bed and just sit in the living room talking and laughing which helped to ease my loneliness with Carl on third shift.

"Sometimes I wonder if her husband Dominic looks down on my husband because he's not fast-paced like he is or as successful. I hope he isn't forbidding Merry to talk with me thinking that I'll be bad company for her. People are always praising them personally and from the pulpit. No one at church sees us witnessing to our neighbors or at the store. Nor do they see our intense sorrow that we deal with as we miss all three of our girls. I search my heart until I feel so guilty and downtrodden. My earnest prayer is that God can say, 'Well done, thou good and faithful servant' when I bow before Him in Heaven someday."

"If you desire that with all your heart, then God won't let you go astray. You know as well as I do that God knows what you personally need and want before you pray, though prayer is the voice that stirs the heart of God. Don't take Merry's inattention toward you as a slight. But take comfort that, in God's foreknowledge, He brought me into your life to fill that void. I hope anyway..."

"Oh, yes!" Serena exclaimed. "I don't think I could bear life without you. I **do** thank God often for your friendship. There are some verses in the Bible that have concerned me lately. Proverbs 18:17--'He that is first in his own cause seemeth just; but his neighbour cometh and searcheth him.'

"Also, Ecclesiastes 7:23-29 talk about King Solomon's search for wisdom. While he was searching out the reason of things, he wrote that he found more bitter than death the woman, whose heart is snares and nets, and her hands as bands. Verse twenty-eight, the second half reads, '...one man among a thousand have I found; but a woman among all those have I not found.'

"I don't want to be overly sensitive; but I don't want to be a carnal, selfish Christian either. How can I fit more service in for the Lord when I can barely keep up with my nanny job, the apartment and laundry, and limited time with Carl? I cried the last time he attended an all night prayer meeting even though I was glad he wanted to go. I miss him terribly.

"We basically say 'hi' and 'bye' and are exhausted working buddies. Then there are Bethany and the Huffs who are well off financially. Miss Emili told me a month ago that she appreciates couples who are actively involved in local charities and are responsible by waiting to have children like they did...years if need be...until they are debt-free. Bethany said something along the same lines this evening. Where do I fit in, Jerusha? I'd never have had children if those were the prerequisites."

"Serena, you've taken too much on yourself.

You have to stop living like this. It isn't healthy. A dear friend of mine died of breast cancer from worrying just like you. She admitted to me that she should have focused on the Lord alone.

"My pastor says, 'You may be able to please some people some of the time, but you will never be able to please all people all of the time.' You mentioned what the Bible calls the 'strange woman.' In Proverbs chapter seven, David's son Solomon also talks about her. She's referred to as being a flatterer. One that speaks words she doesn't mean in order to get her way. She's deceitful. She's stubborn and loud--loving to be out of the house having fun."

Jerusha steered the car onto the exit ramp. "There's another woman in the New Testament that you know all about. Her name was Mary, the sister of Lazarus and Martha. Her priority was to focus solely on the Lord, laying aside the fear of people as the Bible states in Proverbs 29:25. 'The fear of man bringeth a snare.' She willingly honored Him by pouring a pound of costly spikenard ointment on His head and feet while he was eating at a leper's home. There could have been the concern of contracting leprosy herself by going there...along with social stigma. Most of the respected leaders and chief priests consulted about how to put Jesus to death, so Jesus was not well liked by all.

"Mary had to perform her sacrificial, adoring deed in front of a crowd. The Bible mentions this woman honorably in Matthew and John. Even in Mark, she was written about. The people murmured against her saying that she had wasted what cost about three hundred pence (a year's wages) when she could have given that money to the poor. But Jesus said, 'She hath done what she could: she is come aforehand to anoint my body to the burying.' Then he said that wherever the Gospel would be preached throughout the whole world, her act would be spoken of for a memorial of her. See? We're still talking about her.

"Serena, I believe that you need to rest in the fact that you are doing all that you possibly can and pouring yourself into those activities. God's not angrily expecting you to follow your peers, though you can learn from them sometimes. He wants a relationship with *you*. Your performance isn't measured by others' capabilities or talents but only by your own in Christ. Little things that you do faithfully day after day will become great things. Don't get discouraged, dear. God loves you, and so do I...and Carl, of course! Remember, too, that lovingly caring for your husband and doing all in your power to get your family back together *is* doing the will of God."

When Serena walked in the upstairs door at home, Carl was sitting at the table reading his Bible. He looked up and smiled. "Welcome home. You sure got a lot of overtime today."

Serena hungered for a big bear hug to push out her insecurities. Carl was attentive with his eye contact and words, at least, which was a comfort. She eased herself into one of the rounded chairs. She told him about the day's escapade. "And for some reason, today I've been remembering the discussion I had with Bethany two months ago. She didn't even seem to care about Allegra's death. Instead, she told me about how hard it is being married to an older man that wants her to settle down and have a family. Her way of thinking is foreign to me. She's at liberty to live the life we're fighting for. She has wealth, prestige, and a husband that loves her...yet, she's complaining. I guess it wouldn't hurt as much if she'd at least act like she cares about my loss without hastily explaining it away with a lame, 'It's sad how those things happen. There must be a reason.'

"I know all that, but it still doesn't keep me from missing Allegra fiercely. Oh, Carl, if that's how calloused physicians grow, I thank God more than ever that I didn't marry one or aspire to become one."

Carl reached under the table and pulled out a bright blue translucent, inflatable ottoman.

"Try out this foot stool, 'Rena, before I show you some other surprises."

Serena's mouth dropped open as her brain scrambled for an answer. It wasn't her birthday or any other special occasion. She bent down to remove her shoes. Carl had blown air into the cushion until it was nearly tight. The slack he had left allowed her feet to sink in slightly without slipping off. "This provides nearly instant relief, Carl!" she exclaimed in response to his bright, anticipating eyes. You are so sweet!"

"I tried it out myself to see how it felt. Will it do for now, Honey? As soon as we can, I'd like you to consult with the doctor who treats varicose veins with lasers. I've talked to a guy at work whose mother had laser surgery performed recently with excellent results. If only I could afford it NOW."

"Please, Carl," Serena responded sincerely. "This is terrific, and I can enjoy it much more than I'd enjoy something you'd be going into more debt for. How could you even afford this?"

"I received my Thanksgiving/Christmas bonus today. What a surprise that was! Now for the next thing..."

"Oh, Carl! I'll be disappointed if you spent more of this unexpected money. I want it to go on bills. That's why I give you almost every penny of what I earn."

Somewhat apprehensively he replied, "I didn't think you'd mind drinking a milkshake while we watch a movie together."

Serena was puzzled again. "You bought a TV and VCR?" She asked incredulously.

"No," Carl said simply. His smile wasn't as big, but his lips still struggled not to curve higher. "My coworker Bryan was giving away a free TV/DVD combo since he bought a new flat screen set-up. I stopped by the library, before Lucinda's, and got a few movies. I thought you'd enjoy a snack without having to bake one, so I ordered a milkshake for you as I was finishing the mopping. I hope you like it. I had the waitress add syrup flavor shots."

Serena lifted her feet off the plastic ottoman and stood up quickly. Rushing to his side, she bent down and kissed his cheek. "Honey, thank you!"

Carl pushed his way up, too, and led her over to the phone on the dented wall. "Now...the best thing of all." Then he pressed the large playback button on the answering machine.

"Hi, Daddy and Mommy," Joelle said cheerily. "Grandma said that we could call you and leave a message. We just got back from our field trip to the cider mill with Grandma. We watched the men make it, and we got to drink some and eat donut holes."

Brookelle spoke in a wobbly voice. "I miss

you, Mommy and Daddy. I saved a donut for you, and Grandma said that she'll mail it."

Joelle hurried to say, "I love you!"

Brookelle began to cry as she added, "Me, too." The words came out in a fast blurt before the sobs overtook her.

Then Serena's mom concluded the conversation. "Oh, dear! We meant this call to be a happy one. The girls really are doing well. They just miss you, of course, as do Dad and I. Perhaps if you'd both speak on the machine, then we all can hear your voices whenever we call. The girls are terrific blessings and fill our house with joy. Remember that we love you. We'll call again soon. Goodbye."

Serena stood frozen in discouragement as the ending tone beeped. When would they ever be reunited and come to the end of this long valley? Carl turned toward her, embracing her as his warm tears splashed onto her cheek. Guilt swept over her like numbing medication at the dentist's. Tingles prickled her face, down her arms and hands. She hadn't loved him unconditionally. She had blinded herself to the anguish he felt as well.

Jerusha's words from several months ago replayed in her mind. *Carl might feel unworthy of you or mad at himself for having let you down financially. He doesn't want to reward himself with pleasurable times with you until he can prove himself and make things up to you. He's probably emotionally and physically exhausted.*

Serena had questioned, *Well, doesn't he realize that part of proving himself is still reassuring me that he loves and needs me?*

She could still see Jerusha's lips pressed into a straight line. *Probably not, Honey. Hard as it is, he needs your reassurance. Men aren't always as strong as we think them to be. This is where your wedding vows come in. You are his helpmeet, and it's up to you to help him be strong where he lacks.*

But I don't want to push my affections on him and aggravate him, Serena said defensively.

I know it may not be easy, Serena; but you have to let him know that he's worth the risk of allowing yourself to be pushed away. As the Bible says, "Great peace have they that love thy law and nothing shall offend them."

Serena took a deep breath and relaxed against her husband's strong frame. She squeezed him close and let him cry it out. She didn't care how wet her hair got if only the tears were glimmers of healing balm. Carl seemed to sense her emotional state and snuggled her closer against him.

After they were both spent and the tears stopped falling, Serena retrieved the box of tissues, handing him several before blowing her nose. "Carl," she said, looking him directly in the eyes. "You have no idea how much your frugality and thoughtfulness mean to me. You didn't rush out and spend all your money, but you bought the practical stool and the milkshake to prove your love for me. That means more to me than the fanciest, most quality piece of furniture. I can hardly wait to drink the milkshake. I'll split it with you." She smiled up at him with love light shining in her eyes.

"No thank you. That is all yours. I get things at work sometimes. And just so you know, I deposited the rest of the money. I wrote higher amounts on the checks to send out with the bills this month."

Serena said sincerely, "Thank you, Carl. Thank you."

Before going to bed later, Carl read Proverbs 21 to her. Then he prayed the first verse out loud, "'The king's heart is in the hand of the LORD, as the rivers of water: he turneth it whithersoever he will.' God," he said, "You can change our circumstances, but please turn these trials into blessings by the way we accept them. We know the Christian life isn't supposed to be easy, but You promise that You'll reward obedience. Thank you for giving me a wife who stands beside me through thick and thin. If not for me, reward us for her sake, please!"

As they lay there in the darkness, Carl told her some more good news.

Chapter Nine

The Amazing Offer and Decision

Serena told Jerusha on the way to work the next day about the girls' message. "If only we could have called them back, but they would have been in bed much earlier. Also, Carl had some good news about our vehicle situation finally," she ended with a sigh. "Last night was something of a joyful mystery. It seemed too good to be true to have so many surprises at one time. A man at work drives right past Lucinda's Diner on his way home from work. He offered to take Carl every evening that he works there. I'll only need to carpool with you on the off days so he'll have a way home without waiting for me. I'll be able to take him to work in the mornings."

"Who will get him late at night, though, after

he's through at Lucinda's?" Jerusha wondered.

Trying to sound nonchalant, Serena answered, "I'll just go get him." She hurried on, "It appears that two others that Carl works with have been talking with him about vehicles. The one has always wanted a truck, and he'll gladly trade his station wagon for Carl's truck. He'll pay the money, as well, to have the truck repaired as part of an even swap. The station wagon will give us adequate room for our entire family once we're reunited. Carl says that my car that he's been using could give out anytime, too. He's used a powerful compound that is supposed to permanently glue broken parts together. He'd feel unsafe allowing me to drive it alone should anything happen. The other guy at work said that he needs a beater car for his paper route in the mornings. He'll pay Carl one hundred dollars for it and drive it until it dies. He was looking for something that would save wear and tear on his family car. And, Jerusha, Carl bought me a footstool."

They had arrived at the Huffs' house, so Serena bid her friend goodbye. After five months, she still felt nervous whenever she arrived. She forced herself to open the kitchen door. Emili and the girls stood in front of the table expectantly. Self-consciously, Serena pulled off her shoes. Emili said simply, "Good morning."

Then the twins blurted out in unison, "We want you to live with us! Please say 'yes.'"

A haze swept over Serena. "I'm sorry?" she managed to choke out uncertainly while she waited for an explanation.

"Mr. Huff and I have been discussing your pitiful situation and concluded that your need may be our gain. The girls seem to enjoy your company and have been thriving under your tutelage. If you and your husband are in agreement, we'd like to have a probationary time period where you both may live with us. You would stay in the guest suite, and we'd like for you to home instruct the girls next school year."

Serena couldn't understand this employer. One moment she was upset with her and the next...hospitable, even caring. "Really?" She felt dumbfounded. Then she caught herself. Next year sounded so distant. Did she really want to commit herself that long term? "We couldn't impose on your family's privacy like that. Don't take me wrong, though. I appreciate your exceptional offer."

Emili Huff crossed her arms. "We wouldn't suggest this if we thought it inappropriate. Once I dismiss you each day, you may go to your room. I believe you'll find it spacious enough. The girls will take you up to inspect it. There's no need for an immediate answer. If you decide against this, we will be enrolling the girls in private school; so your services wouldn't be needed next year. Your 'rent' would be the money you'd be saving us from the considerable tuition. Also, if this works out, we are prepared to compensate you with a higher pay scale."

"Please say you will!" the girls squealed.

"Girls!" Miss Emili scolded. "Lower your voices, please; and mind your manners. I must be leaving now. We'll talk more later, Serena." Carrying herself with her normal stately posture, she hurried toward the side entrance where the family's shoes and coats were organized. The girls took Serena's hands and pulled her toward the stairs. She allowed herself to be led into the large room. She had peeked into it before but didn't remember much about its layout or furnishings.

She gasped. The girls climbed up onto the queen bed and watched her slowly tour the beautiful suite. It was as clean as the rest of the three-story house. Serena breathed deeply of the fresh smelling air...unlike the stale smell of the old carpets and rotting cupboards in the apartment. She had become more accustomed to the irritants in such close quarters. The chilly temperatures and inclement weather of the season forced her to keep all the windows shut. The old tobacco smoke and probable animal dander that permeated the rugs, along with mold in the previously neglected, damp cupboards below the leaky sink, had been triggering her allergy and asthma symptoms. She removed her pots and pans one day when she had several hours to spare and had scrubbed the shelves and interior walls with bleach water. Mold is difficult to kill, however; so she endured her asthma symptoms when she was there.

Her parents had always maintained an immaculate home, even laying linoleum that had a pattern like a rag rug in her bedroom. They had faithfully taken her each week for allergy shots and bought her whatever inhalers the doctor prescribed. Then when Carl and Serena were first married, they were in a pleasant rental property before purchasing their home in which Serena was at liberty to rip up old carpeting. Carl had rolled it up and carried it to the curb for her. Then she and their girls, with masks on, hand sanded the rough wood floors and mopped them several times before Serena painted them with a wood stain/polyurethane varnish that she found in the basement. The floors may not have looked great to visitors, but to Serena they looked clean and nice--representing hours of hard work.

Now in the apartment, life wasn't easy. Maybe this proposal of Miss Emili's really was an answer to their prayers. She tiptoed through the bedroom's sitting area with its plush cream-colored carpet. "Oh, look!" she admired, pushing her hands deep into the puffy down-filled comforter.

The girls copied her with big smiles lighting their little faces. "Do you like it, Serena?" They gazed at her so hopefully that Serena couldn't resist hugging them.

"I do." She might have to use her own bedspread if the down aggravated her allergies, but it was beautiful. Then she walked to the far corner and entered the private bathroom. The big, ceramic tiles with mauve, marble swirl felt cool through her socks. Spotless wall mirrors enhanced the good-sized room making it seem even larger. A shiny double-seat shower stall glistened like new on the opposite end. A gray countertop sported two sink bowls that sat underneath which would make cleaning a breeze. She opened up the wooden doors below. To her surprise, the countertop and sinks allowed the vanity lights to shine through. She had never seen anything like it before. It sure was easier to see things. A large frosted window on the outside wall brightened the cheery lavatory even more.

Returning to the bedroom, her eyes swept over the entire area. There was an oversized burgundy recliner beside another window. The vacuum brush had left the suede looking soft and neat. It was separated from a matching love seat by a glossy walnut end table. A glass-globed lamp with etched roses and golden feet was the only thing on it. The starkness was refreshing after the cramped apartment living. Miss Emili had been right. It was spacious. Soft, velour pillows smothered the little couch along with a new throw. Beyond the double seat stood a lacy floor arrangement of artificial ferns.

Serena's attention was drawn to a subtle painting of a meandering path, lined with young trees, through a floral park. She wandered toward the large oak desk that was set at an angle just inside near the hall. A large dark green sofa and table and chairs completed the array. Serena sat down on the couch.

The girls came bounding over. "What? Is everything okay?"

"Why do you ask?"

"Because you sighed."

"Oh! Did I? It was a happy one. This suite is delightful! Don't get excited until I talk this over with my husband. In the meantime, we'd best get busy. I want to show your mother that I'm grateful for her offer and will be the best worker I can possibly be."

One month later when their lease expired, Carl and Serena were in the back of a store waiting for an employee to bring out some egg boxes to use for packing when Serena spotted some candy canes. "Oh, Carl! I've been wishing we could be a witness to our neighbors somehow before we move. We've been so busy with work that we haven't had time to get acquainted, and I haven't had time to bake goodies to take over. Please may we buy candy canes for them?"

"Honey, I don't know. Wouldn't it seem kind of silly to hand them a box of candy canes?"

"Well, I thought we'd be a little more tactful in our presentation. A group of three, perhaps, tied up with a ribbon."

The worker pushed through the double doors pulling a laden cart behind him. "Will this do?"

Carl turned toward him. "Yes, and thank you."

"Thank you! You just saved me a chunk of time, so I won't have to break these down."

Serena had been looking in her purse and shyly stepped over. She extended her hand that held a small folded paper with a nativity scene on the front. "Merry Christmas, Sir. This is a tract about how you may know for sure that you're on your way to Heaven according to the Bible, God's Word. All of us have sinned and fall short of getting there on our own. My husband and I have accepted Jesus' forgiveness, and we've never once regretted our personal decisions."

The man held the paper uncertainly.

Carl explained, "It's yours to keep, and we'd love to have you attend our church over the holidays, though where a person attends church isn't the most important thing."

The man took it, mumbling a thank you. "Hope your move goes smoothly," he said as he walked away.

Carl took hold of the cart handle. "I guess I'll take these out to the station wagon."

"Honey, what about the candy canes?"

"Go ahead and pick some out."

"I was hoping to look in the craft section for some red ribbon to tie the candy bouquets with."

Carl seemed impatient. "Just let me get these in the car."

"Do you want me to go with you or purchase the things on my own?"

"Get them, and I'll pull up to the door when you come out." He started pushing the cart down the aisle.

"Carl, I don't have any cash."

He sighed and backed up--then said, "Actually, I'll come back in and find you; and we'll check out together."

Serena was relieved to shop alone, so she wouldn't frustrate him further. She selected mint and cherry-flavored candy canes before she hurried to find just the right spool of ribbon. Soon Carl was standing beside her.

"You were fast. Of course, I can expect that from you. You are an amazing packer. Remember how the men that helped us move out of our first apartment couldn't get over your organization?"

He smiled, much more relaxed. "I'm sorry for being terse. I guess I just didn't want to walk around the store with a top heavy load of boxes."

"I'm sure you're tired, too," Serena empathized. "How do you think this would look?" She held up red satin ribbon with gilded gold wire edges and some delicate green swirls threaded throughout.

Carl agreed that it would complement the candy, and they headed for the registers that were situated between the grocery section and the department store items. Carl asked for a Christmas tract. "It's my turn to pass one out." He smiled as he took it from Serena's hand and tucked it into his shirt pocket.

The lady at the checkout wasn't as obliging as the other employee. "Ahh," she pretentiously sympathized when Serena added about Allegra's passing. The woman seemed like she despised the use of their recent grief as an "in" to her spiritual condition. But to Serena it felt like an appropriate way to remember by caring for someone else besides wallowing in her own sorrow.

The woman bagged the purchases and held out the plastic handles toward Carl. "Just be glad the manager wasn't up here. He'd escort you out. Solicitors aren't allowed."

Serena smiled cordially. "Ma'am, the dictionary refers to solicitation as persistent asking or someone who especially entreats for charity funding. We are only offering you a completely free paper about eternity because we care."

"Merry Christmas," Carl concluded politely. Serena felt shaky as she held onto his elbow. He led them out into the parking lot. The icy wind bit into her throat and stung her nose. She let go to button the top of her coat.

"Was I too bold?" Serena asked. "Why are people so uncaring about those who have died and even about their own futures?"

Carl reached for her hand and squeezed it as he guided her across the busy crosswalk. Christmas shoppers were out in numbers, and the parking lot was a mass of coming and going cars. They walked briskly toward the station wagon that Serena had managed to clean inside after the vehicle trades Carl made at work. "You contended for the faith, 'Rena. The Bible says to do that, and you held fast the profession of our faith without wavering. Thank you for provoking me unto love and good works even when I don't feel like it. God knew just the help meet I needed."

"Thank you for that. What an honor to know that God counted me worthy to work through difficult times with you." She spoke slowly through her teeth, clenching her jaws, to keep them from chattering.

As they neared the light blue and fake wood paneled vehicle, Carl said, "I left the doors unlocked since I knew we'd be out shortly and we don't have anything to steal besides the jumper cables and radio."

"I'm so glad." Serena concentrated on tensing her muscles, so her body wouldn't shake. Carl opened the door for her in his gentlemanly way and waited patiently while she climbed in out of the gusts. After he shut the door, she blew on her hands. Powdery snowflakes caught in Carl's dark hair while he walked around the car.

Blowing in breathlessly, he shut the door and shoved the key into the ignition at the same moment. "The faster this engine warms up, the sooner we'll have heat."

Serena pressed her knees together hoping they wouldn't shake. Once Carl had maneuvered through the traffic and the car had grown toasty, Serena wondered aloud. "Carl, what if we wrote our own tract about how we got saved and mention Allegra and how calming it is to know where she is? We could hand those out with the candy canes."

Carl glanced at the radio clock. "The library should still be open. We can design something there and pay to use the printer for one original. Then I can stop at the office supply store tomorrow evening and run off copies. We shouldn't need more than ten should we?"

"No." Serena quickly unbuckled and scooted over beside him. The carpeted hump that separated the driver's side from the passenger's was low and wide enough that her feet were able to rest comfortably on it. She fastened the middle seat belt firmly and smiled at Carl's puzzled expression. "This feels like a date."

A discreet smile tugged at his lips. Then Serena asked urgently, "Can we be fast, though? I'm longing something fierce to talk with our girls." The passion in her voice was so strong that it startled even herself. "The times that I am able to talk with them are few and far between. I feel homesick. It's like I'm leading a stranger's life..." Her voice broke as she struggled to stay in control of her emotions.

Carl squeezed her hand and held it as he drove single-handed. "Why don't we go home directly? You can call your parents' before it gets any later. I'll make coffee while you're talking, and then we can sit down together and write up our tract. Then, if you trust my judgment, I can go to the library on my own tomorrow. I can get to the office store on Saturday and still have the tracts ready to hand out before we move."

Serena couldn't speak, but she hoped her eyes portrayed how she felt as she gazed at him.

The girls were brushing their teeth, so Serena's mom talked for a few minutes first. "I can only imagine how you feel, Sweetie. Try not to punish yourself, though. In some ways, I think it's easier that they don't talk with you that often. When they do, they're somber for a few days afterwards.

"The thank you note and stickers you sent a while back for the cookies the girls baked—and the doughnuts--meant more than you know. They still take turns sleeping with them. They won't even use the stickers because they want the sheet of them to be a memento. Serena, Dad and I can't get over your creativity in cleaning up the other twins' dolls that you discovered in the trash. You made them look like new. The girls treat them like royalty, and we never told them where you obtained them. Oh, here are the girls. I'll put them on speaker phone."

"Mommy!" they squealed in unison.

"Are you rich now so we can live with you again?" Brookelle asked.

"No, darlin'," Serena answered regretfully.

"But, Mommy, how could you buy those expensive dolls for us?" Joelle wondered.

Serena choked back the tears that flooded her throat. "I...didn't buy them. God...He...provided them. They just needed Mommy to be a nurse and fix them up a little. It's Mommy's secret, okay?"

"Okay," they both responded. "We miss you." They spoke in unison again...which always proved to Serena that they were identical twins. They weren't just sisters. They were part of each other.

"I miss you, too," she said with deep feeling. "I wish that I could hug you both and bring you home tonight! We're working very hard to make that possible. "Please keep calling and leaving us messages...and pray. Hearing your voices is what I live for. Are you being good for Grandpa and Grandma? Are you doing well on your schoolwork? Maybe you can send me some of your pages."

Serena hung up the phone weakly.

Carl jumped up from the futon. "Serena," he said, "I have been struggling with the decision to move into the Huffs' home. I know I said that we could, but I haven't had any peace today.

I read my Bible over lunch break and gave my lunch to a guy that had forgotten his. I felt convicted to pray and fast. While I worked, I prayed and prayed silently. I begged God for guidance. Then I remembered that you had put a Bible CD in my lunch box a while ago. I had set it in my toolbox at the shop. I got it out and listened to it the rest of the day.

"Before I tell you the verse that seemed to be specifically for me, let me preface it with some information. The other day, your dad left a message on my cell phone. He was glad about our opportunity, but he wanted us to consider moving up with them temporarily until we're on our feet again and find work and housing up there. He and your mom didn't want us to be in a rush to get back to them, but they wanted us to consider it. I asked God about that question in particular."

Serena sat down on the futon and gave him her undivided attention while Carl paced the floor. She hadn't seen him this excited in a long time. There was a new spark in his eyes, and she thought she knew how he had decided. Remaining quiet, she began to smile...unable to hide her growing hope.

Carl's voice grew louder. "When the man on the CD read Acts 11:12, I felt like jumping up and shouting. 'And the spirit bade me go with them, nothing doubting. Moreover these six brethren accompanied me, and we entered into the man's house.' Do you get that?" Carl looked straight into Serena's eyes.

She hopped up to hug him. "When can we go?"

"As soon as I can get *six* men lined up to help us load our things here and from the storage unit into a rental truck." Carl beamed at her reaction.

"What about our jobs? I mean, are we just going to walk away from the little bit of income we do have?"

"Serena, believe me, I know how you feel. That's why I labored in prayer today. Let me show you what I read in my Bible over lunch break. I was reading in Deuteronomy chapter eight." He flipped to it skillfully. "Here it is. 'And thou shalt remember all the way which the LORD thy God led thee...in the wilderness, to humble thee, and to prove thee, to know what was in thine heart, whether thou wouldest keep his commandments, or no..that he might make thee know that man doth not live by bread only, but by every word that proceedeth out of the mouth of the LORD doth man live. Therefore thou shalt keep the commandments of the LORD thy God, to walk in his ways, and to fear him.'"

"So you're saying, 'Do we live what we believe', right?"

"Yes," Carl answered. "It may be an adventure, but this isn't exactly a fun one here is it?"

Serena shook her head. "I was concerned about always being in the Huffs' house. We wouldn't have much privacy. I kept trying to tell myself what Pastor Eclant preached recently about pride. Do you remember how he said, 'Don't cause baby Christians to stumble or be offended, and be a good testimony. But, don't fret and be worrying what people think about you. Everyone isn't always thinking about us anyway. We aren't really all that important.' I memorized the text he used. John 3:30- 'He must increase, but I must decrease.'"

Carl pulled her close and said against her hair, "Let's just do what we can; and if God opens the doors, we'll continue to walk through them."

Chapter Ten

An Aspiring Dream

At church on Sunday, Carl and Serena were there earlier than they usually were. Stephen arrived at the same time and walked with them to the door. He had the church key and let them all in. "I was hoping to have a chance to talk with you this morning," he informed them. He flipped the latch into the door, so it wouldn't lock when it shut behind them. Others were bound to arrive any minute.

He flipped on the lights in the lobby then in the auditorium, and they walked up front. "I learned about something at my competition that I thought you might be interested in." He looked directly at Serena. "I know it'd depend on Carl's approval; but I can tell how much you enjoy music and the piano, like I do. Well, there's a contest in New York that I believe I've mentioned to you before.   I found out it could provide a nice paycheck if you were a winner. I picked up an entry form for you.   There's just some basic information you must fill out before mailing it in."

"Don't I lack qualifications?   I mean I haven't gone through music school like you."

"I know," Stephen replied, "but you had an excellent teacher that did.   This competition's purpose is to find masters of the art who have succeeded by hard work and talent to be an encouragement to others who are less fortunate. I even brought you a stamp to mail the paper out." Stephen looked at Carl as he pulled it from his shirt pocket.

Carl rewarded him with a reassuring smile before Stephen handed it to Serena. She felt as if she were physically holding hope in her hands. "Thank you, Stephen, for thinking of me like this," she said softly around the lump in her throat.

"How did your competition go?" Carl wondered.

"It was the most entertaining one yet," he remarked, smiling at the memory. "We contestants had all filled out a form, something like yours, at the registration several weeks prior.   We had to check from a multiple choice which composer's music was the most foreign to us. Just before we went up to play, we were handed a three-page selection of one of that composer's works. Each piece of music was different from each other's, but they were all selected to be just the same level. The judges watched us and kept score on how well we could sight read without looking down at our hands.

"The crowded room was hot, so someone opened a window behind the piano. I had just spread my music out on the rack and proceeded halfway into one of the pages when suddenly a gust of wind sucked at the screenless window and drew the paper up over my head and outside. It startled me so that I completely stopped, probably looking very dumbfounded. The crowd roared with amusement.

"After a few moments, I regained my sense of bearings and thought to close the window and start over by ear, composing by turn until I made my way into the second page. The applause was thunderous when I finished; and after the competition, I was enjoying a big lifesaver when several of the judges started walking toward me. Somehow I accidentally swallowed it, and it lodged in my throat. I felt like I were choking, but I didn't want them to know since I had already made a spectacle of myself.

"I just smiled at them as they spoke; and when it was my turn to respond, I could only point to my throat and mouth words. "Please excuse me." I hurried to the water fountain and drank for a while, hoping it'd dissolve. The Lord sure has a unique way of keeping us humble."

On Monday night, Jerusha and Serena went to the Laundromat. The parking lot was full. Serena hated going there, but Jerusha's company made the lack of privacy more bearable. Jerusha opened the car hatch, and Serena grasped their heavy laundry bags. Pressing her lips into a straight line, she followed Jerusha...reminding herself that she had just as much business to be there as anyone else. The other patrons were as vulnerable as she.

A talk show was blaring on the mounted television, and all the chairs were taken. Several women looked over at them. Serena smiled out of habit. One at the end of the row smiled vaguely, but the others either raised their eyebrows or just turned back toward the TV. Even if Ohioans considered themselves to be Southerners, they hadn't learned Southern hospitality yet.

She grew more and more awkward as she walked down the aisles around carts, hampers and baskets. She found two empty washers separated by a man putting clothes in the middle machine. Serena wished they could leave and find an emptier place, but she knew there wasn't another one as clean as this nearby. Every time she was here, the Vietnamese woman made her rounds wiping out empty washing machines with bleach water. Serena always tried to reassure herself that the dryers' heat would also kill lurking germs.

She also felt safer here because employees worked behind the dry cleaners' desk. She had been to strictly coin-operated locations before where she had been left alone with some shady characters. Serena had no choice but to lock herself in the car until they left before she'd return for her dry clothes.

Setting her bag on the floor, she stayed far to the right of her washer away from the man. Thankful that she had pre-sorted at home, she began discreetly hiding more personal articles behind other laundry as she filled the washer. Hopefully the lady had just disinfected it. What choice did she have without the convenience of one at the apartment?

She certainly did not want to wear her clothes so many times that she'd be known for having body odor. Elderly people frequently seemed to reminisce about how difficult and frugal their lives had been. Serena believed that it was one thing in pioneer days to have only two dresses, but she lived in the here and now. The same country but with a different culture...and she had no intentions of misrepresenting the Lord by being offensive. It was a pet peeve of hers when older people tried to make the younger generations feel guilty for having life so posh. It was no one's choice to decide when to be born.

In some ways, she found it difficult not to envy the old days' down-home, slower pace. Without electricity, they had longer nights of sleep...*early to bed, early to rise* way of life like she had read about in Laura Ingalls Wilder's books as a child. It was funny to her how the older people would complain about the outrageous prices of the here and now, yet they talked up their meager grocery money in years past. Didn't they realize that the smaller amount of money stretched farther then? They ate more wholesome, homegrown food, too.

She wasn't naive, however. She'd read about the hardships as well, but she longed for the simpler times of family and community...spelling bees, pie contests and neighborly caring. She ached like she was homesick for her husband to work in nearby fields. She may never know what it would be like for her and the children to freely go to him with a question or to drink some cold liquor-free eggnog in the open outdoors.

She yearned to be free from the modern trap of debt...despite its being largely unintentional on their part. It was a heavenly dream to imagine taking charge of the multiple distractions like telephones and even easy travel which could make life crazy because so much more was expected of people. The postal service and rules of etiquette left no excuses for the lack of thank you notes...no matter how sincere the verbal words of gratitude. Long walks, like they used to take, were no longer possible due to lack of time.

Sometimes she felt like respectfully answering the aged critics when they'd conglomerate all younger generations into one spoiled group. "Quite frankly, Sir or Ma'am, I enjoy several mile walks. The birds' twittering in the spring, the fragrant flowers in the summer, the crunchy leaves tumbling along the ground in the fall, and the nippy air against my face in the winter are medicinal to me. Your walks to school must have given you time to think, helped you enjoy your meals and kept you trim."

Serena poured the blue detergent over the laundry and shoved the quarters in. "Excuse me," she said to the man as she made her way around him. He was leaning against his machine since there were still no available seats.

"Sure," he replied absently. His eyes were fixed on the TV, and he was chomping on pretzels. He held a can of grape soda. Condensation dripped down his hand and onto the floor. Suddenly Serena realized how warm she had become...and how thirsty.

Jerusha had finished up at her washer and came over while Serena finished starting the second washer. "How about going for a walk on the plaza's sidewalk and getting a drink?"

"Yes," Serena promptly agreed. "Only it will be my treat since you treated me last to the Mexican restaurant." Even if her clothes couldn't fully dry because of using several of the laundry quarters, she would be polite and not always be a sponge. She'd just drape the damp things over furniture at home until they air dried, if need be.

There was a drop of several degrees when they stepped outside. As they passed an antique shop's window, Serena spotted a black rectangular sign that read, 'Simplify.' So much wisdom compressed into one plain word. She would have bought it to be her motto if she could have.

Jerusha spotted a large straw hat that reminded her of her mother's gardening hat since it had a large rim to protect her face and neck from the sun. It even had tassels dangling from the edges to keep insects at bay whenever she moved.

"I've thought about a hat for my dining room ever since we ate out and admired the Mexicans' decor." Then they entered the small grocery and browsed as they wandered toward the refrigerated sections. The prices were much better than the vending machines' back at the cleaners', but Serena still had to count out the few quarters she could spare and then added lots of pennies to make the difference. She felt like an eager schoolchild whose money burned holes in her pocket.

After they returned and switched their clothes to the dryers, Jerusha offered to drive over to the cemetery that was fairly close. The flowers were thriving by Allegra's and Mrs. Shelby's graves. After Serena finished her pop, she pulled the weeds and filled the empty can at the spigot nearby. She watered the plants then settled back down on Jerusha's picnic blanket.

Jerusha studied the small headstone thoughtfully and asked, "How did you choose Allegra's name?"

"I first thought about it when I read the poem 'The Children's Hour' by Henry Wadsworth Longfellow. 'Laughing Allegra' matched my love of music and the term 'allegro.' Now she is happy with God. How can anyone make it through life's sorrows without Christ, Jerusha? I'll never know."

They pulled into the parking lot just as Jerusha's watch alarm sounded. "Well, I guess our clothes should be dry."

They each carried their clean baskets inside. Serena stuck a gospel tract in the smallest one in case she had an opportunity to hand it to someone that she'd speak with. When they walked through the door, only a couple of the same people were there. Many new customers had taken their places. Nearing the droning dryers, Serena saw her laundry in a cart. Two ladies stood in front of it. A plump woman, who bustled around the place as if she were the owner, briskly approached her. She began talking as she walked. "I took your loads out after waiting half an hour. I really needed the dryers."

"Really?" Serena questioned, puzzled for a moment. "But the dryers should have stopped just a few minutes ago."

The woman hurried away and began setting quarters into slots on several washers before shoving all the little change drawers in. Then she rushed out to a pickup truck that had backed up to the door and brought in more overstuffed laundry bags. Serena assumed then that she must work for a bed and breakfast or small hotel. She asked the ladies by her laundry to please excuse her and pulled the cart out from behind them.

She hoped her clothes were dry enough and that this woman hadn't used some of the time she had paid for. It was disconcerting to know that a complete stranger had touched what she'd wear. She tried to comfort herself that she'd be at others' mercies if she were sleeping elsewhere on vacation with Carl. Everything seemed to be in the cart, so she shook the wrinkles out before laying the clothes in her laundry baskets. She and Jerusha always folded at home. Serena felt badly about not having been more understanding to the woman. If she had been more sociable, she may have had the opportunity to give her the tract. Now she was behind the counter talking with the Vietnamese woman. Jerusha was ready, so Serena left with her.

Chapter Eleven

Saying Goodbye

On Tuesday, Carl and Serena bundled up in their winter wear. Serena held the candy bouquets, and Carl locked the door before turning and holding out his arm for her. Merry, from church, had given her the boots she wore. They hadn't fit her well, she had said, and began to chafe after she had thrown the receipt away. Serena was grateful to have stylish, new dress boots. They had two-inch heels and fit okay if she wore socks over her stockings. The soles' grips weren't very effective on the ice, but Serena wanted to represent the Lord with a well-groomed freshness.

She gripped the inside of Carl's arm, just above his elbow. "You have the tracts then?"

"I sure do," he assured her, opening his unzipped coat for her to see them sticking out of the inside pocket.

Serena smiled appreciatively. "You did a fabulous job."

Carl led her across the street first. They had bought just enough candy canes for the closest surrounding neighbors that were at least acquaintances. They'd see each other and wave or call out "hellos" going to and from work. The first guy, with long hair, that answered Carl's firm knock seemed polite. "Happy holidays to you, too. Good luck with your move." He took the tract Carl offered to him and one of the bouquets from Serena. "Thanks. I haven't had a candy cane yet this year."

The next place was an upstairs apartment in another of the city's old, rambling houses. The clean looking woman in her late twenties was professional at first until Carl explained that along with the treat was a paper explaining how they had come to know Christ as their personal Saviour. She suddenly turned rudely cold and swore before exclaiming, "I don't believe this!" She ignored Carl's outstretched hand and slammed the door in their faces. They could hear her yelling on purpose to be overheard, "That's what I hate!"

Serena squeezed Carl's arm as they carefully made their way back down the wooden staircase. The female that greeted them at the downstairs apartment had the most forbidding appearance. Her clothing was all black, and she had earrings all over. Her hair was highlighted in several contrasting shades, and she had plenty of makeup. Carl was as sincere with her as he had been with the others. "Hello. My name is Carl, and this is my wife Serena. We really regret that we haven't had the opportunity to officially meet you before this, but we wanted to wish you a merry Christmas before we move."

"How nice! What a creative idea…bouquets made of candy," the woman said affably. "Please come in out of the cold." She opened the door wider. Carl stepped aside so Serena could lead the way in. A large, lighted aquarium, filled with many different fish, was centered on the main living room wall beneath a three-dimensional underwater painting. Serena counted three cats right off the bat. She felt a sneeze coming, and pressed a gloved hand under her nose. She managed to stifle it though her eyes began itching.

The young lady said, "My name is Carli. I've seen you both coming and going, and I've seen you carrying in egg boxes and wondered if you'd be leaving." She didn't seem the least bit ashamed of her observances. Serena appreciated her unpretentious manner. "When and where are you moving?"

Serena spoke this time. "On Thursday, we'll be moving back to the State of New York, where we both grew up, to be near family." She smiled warmly at their neighbor.

"You're braver than I'd be," she said with an incredulous note in her voice. "I need space from my family."

Serena started to expound upon the tract when the phone rang.

The neighbor concluded, "I'm so glad you came over. It was great to have met you. Have a good Christmas, and I hope your move goes well."

"Goodbye," they answered, tucking the paper beneath the candy canes on the coffee table. Serena and Carl let themselves out as she went to answer the phone. They crossed the littered street and climbed onto the porch of the man who lived below them. Serena shivered, and Carl reached up to rap the old-fashioned doorknocker, but the door opened.

"Yes?" wondered a sleepy voice as a puff of cigarette smoke floated into their faces. Then the man stuck his head out. He took everything they gave him but seemed in a hurry to get the door shut.

Carl said, "We'll let you go so we don't freeze you and heat the outdoors."

"Glad you came," the quiet man answered. "If I knew I was going to have company, I wouldn't still be lounging in my p.j.'s. I apologize." Serena was surprised by his proper speech and manners despite his appearance and smoking. She had always been uncomfortable outside when he was sitting on the rickety porch watching her. Perhaps she had misjudged him because of his seeming curiosity about their lives.

When they returned to their apartment, Serena and Carl were relieved that every neighbor they had hoped to speak with had been home. Serena thanked Carl for his willingness.

"I'm glad we did it, too," he agreed. He took her hands and began to pray. "Lord, we prayed before we went out; but we wish to thank You now for answered prayer and ask You to please work in our neighbors' hearts to want to accept You as their Saviour." Then they packed their meager belongings, carefully deciding what to leave out for the next two days. Three men from work and three from church were planning to help.

Wednesday was difficult. Serena drove alone to the Huffs' to take them and Barb and Dan some homemade rolls she had baked as farewell gifts. The girls acted hurt that she'd desert them and kept their distance. Miss Emili was cordial and wished her well, thanking her for her excellent work. On the way out, though, Dan and Barb met Serena on the sidewalk in tears. Barb hugged her tightly, and Dan shook her hand—squeezing it.

"You've become very special to us," Barb spoke for them both, Dan nodding his head as he read her lips. "Please don't ever change. You've been a breath of fresh air to this house."

"Thank you, both. I love you and enjoyed working around you. God was good to allow me the privilege of meeting you two." She began to choke up. A biting wind began to tug at them. The temperature seemed to be dropping quickly. The wintry chill froze the tears in her sinuses into what felt like icy needles. Her toes and fingertips felt numb. The three of them grasped their coats close against their throats and nodded their goodbyes. Serena hurried to the station wagon.

At the next stop, Serena fought the wind to open the back car door and retrieved a large gift bag she had bought at a dollar-type store. It contained a second-hand straw hat that looked like new, adorned with crisp-looking red and yellow ribbons and flowers that would match Jerusha's modern, bold decorating style. At home, Serena had put it in a paper bag and poured salt over it. Rolling the bag's top down several times, she shook it vigorously to remove any dust. Then she took the hat back out and carefully spot checked it with a thin, damp rag.

For Bethany, she had chosen her favorite book about marriage that had often encouraged her during their struggles. She felt chagrin over having to part with it, but she couldn't afford a new one. It would be worth the sacrifice if it'd help another couple as well. She had wiped it and flipped through it before wrapping it neatly in a clean section of a paper grocery sack she had cut out. She tied it firmly with some purple-colored twine from Allegra's bead jewelry kit. She consoled herself that, after all, the Bible was the book she should be reading most since it contained all the answers.

Trying not to crunch the gifts against her as the stiff breeze whipped at them, she pushed hard at the door. It finally gave beneath her hand and closed. Bethany and Jerusha greeted her at the kitchen entrance. Bethany's feminine, carefree-sounding laughter whirled around until Serena could shut the door. No acquaintances would realize that beneath this stylish, successful doctor's contagious affability were discontent and selfishness.

"Why don't we sit in the living room and open these?" Bethany suggested.

"Thank you," Serena hastened, "but I don't have much time, and I prefer your homey kitchen...perhaps because I bake a lot."

The ladies each opened the presents, and Bethany embraced Serena loosely. "You haven't changed a bit, dear. You're still giving 'Rena. Sweetie, not to offend you, of course, but you know how busy doctors can be. I'd only waste it by setting it on a shelf. I hope you understand," she soothed, looking apologetic but firm at the same time.

"I'm sure you are extremely busy," Serena said, "but you never know when you may have some free time. This book is the best I've read on marriage and why bad things can happen to us. It talks about how God can prove to Satan and other people that a righteous person will be faithful to Him regardless. He displays His power more in our times of weakness if we lean on God. The author reminds that disease, accidents and natural disasters can befall any of us. I thank God every day that Carl is still with me.

"The book also highlights the life of Joseph in the Bible. It puts a fresh light on his sufferings since I normally hear preaching about Job—though not to belittle his calamities at all! Joseph's character was tested and ultimately strengthened. One might expect persecution from the world but not by family. Joseph had two strikes against him. His attitude was tested as Pharaoh's chief butler forgot him.

"Joseph's brothers thought he was proud,

and maybe he was a little since his father favored him. So God allowed Joseph who had become unusually blessed in Potiphar's house to be humbled in prison before Joseph would be ready to test and judge his brothers' attitudes when they came to Egypt for food. He didn't rejoice over punishing his brothers but wept instead. When the brothers found out he was the highly exalted ruler, there was no despising then.

"Anyway, this is a fabulous novel with interesting fiction while being filled, obviously, with Biblical examples."

"I guess so. Now, Dear, I picked up two-dozen fresh doughnuts for you from the bakery. Carl and the men will work up appetites. Jerusha separated the varieties and bagged them to keep soft until tomorrow."

Serena opened her eyes wide and exclaimed, "What a thoughtful idea, Bethany! We'll enjoy them." She hoped her smile hid the dejection she felt that her gift hadn't been accepted as gladly.

"You'll have to be sure to send me your new address once you're settled," Bethany said breezily. "Maybe we'll have the opportunity to visit you sometime when we're up there visiting family. Being doctors, though, it's difficult to get much time off."

Serena wished Bethany hadn't tried to be so

polite by mentioning it. "Surely you know my parents' address. It's still the same, if you ever happen to feel inclined." She felt like saying, *You won't come. I'm just your poor friend.* Guilt washed over her as she remembered all she had just said about Joseph. Was she willing to be humbled?

Bethany pecked Serena on the cheek and said, "I really must be leaving for the office."

"Oh, yes. I understand and am grateful you allowed me to keep you this long. I have to go visit the cemetery and run several more errands before church, so I should head out, too."

No empathy flickered in her eyes as she said coolly, "Yes. Good luck, Serena."

Once they were left alone, Jerusha took both of Serena's hands firmly in her own. "If you can, read II Corinthians chapter one before you go to bed tonight, Honey. Keep walking through your valley. And, Serena, I like the wall hat. It will always remind me of you. Please send pictures of you and your precious family reunited. I love you. Just keep praying for Bethany and her husband."

Chapter Twelve

Moving

Saying goodbye to everyone at church on Wednesday night was bittersweet. It was heartbreaking, yet it also showed them how much people really cared that didn't always say much. The church had truly become home away from home for Serena. Sunday and Wednesday services were the highlights of every week. No matter how poor she was, she was accepted and loved. Merry and Dominic had been on deputation for a while, and that helped. She was beginning to come to grips with the fact that God had chosen her to be Carl's one and only helpmeet. She had the seemingly menial task of helping him through financial difficulties. She prayed extra hard before services when missionaries would be visiting that

God would help her not to feel inferior.

Serena went up to the platform to see what list of songs the director had set on the organ. She marked the pages in the hymnbook with sticky notes. While she waited for Stephen to come up and begin playing the prelude, Serena lovingly looked at the organ. She would have been content to attend this church indefinitely unless God would have ever called Carl to serve somewhere else as a preacher or missionary. The people were sincere, and the preaching was as interesting as it could be. God had given Pastor Eclant the talent of teaching Biblical truths clearly.

Serena glanced out over the crowd. To her amazement, she saw their neighbor, who lived below them, sitting in the last row. Serena hurried back to the pew where Carl was sitting; and, together, they walked back to greet him. He was clean-shaven, had a fresh haircut and was dressed like an executive. Serena almost wouldn't have recognized him if it weren't for his piercing eyes. She wondered how he could afford those clothes, let alone know how to dress so stately. She had thought he was poor like they were, but that only proved her and Carl's situation even more. They were poor; but out and around, they wore their well-fitting, clean and ironed clothing that still looked crisp. No one had to know that they were wearing hand-me-downs or clothes bought from the Salvation Army.

"I'm Jim," he said simply. "Carl...Serena, how can I ever thank you enough for stopping by my apartment? My sister-in-law has been after me for three years to get saved. I just couldn't believe something as simple as believing and asking Jesus into my heart would really work. It wasn't polite, I know; but I often watched your coming and going. You always seemed cheerful and loving to each other when you were going through hard times. I noticed that you had two vehicles, and one broke down. You never replaced it but carpooled and got by with one.

"I also read your bumper sticker several times while I sat on the porch. 'Let us hear the conclusion of the whole matter: Fear God, and keep his commandments: for this is the whole duty of man.' I had never thought much about why I'm here on Earth or Who made me. That's a pretty powerful statement that got me pondering, especially since my wife Jeannie died a year ago. I got saved last night, and followed the little map on the back of the paper you gave me to come tonight."

"Congratulations, Jim!" Carl said, gently slapping him on the back. "That's the best decision you'll ever make."

Serena smiled and nodded before excusing herself to return to the organ. Stephen was already playing. As soon as Serena took her seat on the bench, the song service began.

Serena and Carl were scheduled to sing a duet; so after the offering, she walked over to the piano and adjusted the microphone as Stephen went down. Carl sang a low tenor part in his rich bass voice. "I hear the Savior say, 'Thy strength indeed is small! Child of weakness, watch and pray, Find in Me thine all in all.'"

Serena joined in on the chorus singing the alto part. "Jesus paid it all, All to Him I owe; Sin had left a crimson stain--He washed it white as snow." Then she sang the third verse solo. "For nothing good have I Whereby Thy grace to claim--I'll wash my garments white In the blood of Calv'ry's Lamb." Again, they sang together. Only this time, Carl sang the harmony deep and low. "Jesus paid it all, All to Him I owe; Sin had left a crimson stain--He washed it white as snow." They slowly repeated the chorus once more, singing it with all their hearts.

It was difficult for Serena to rest during the preaching. They were moving tomorrow, and Jim wouldn't have Carl around to disciple him. She wished they could have invited him up to the apartment for a snack or afforded to take him out.

Pastor Eclant's text was Philippians 1:6—"Being confident of this very thing, that He which hath begun a good work in you will perform it until the day of Jesus Christ." He reminded them that it's only by God's mercy that they, including himself, were able to be faithful to Him. "Not by might, nor by power, but by my spirit, saith the LORD of hosts." Zechariah 4:6 (the last half)

Then he referenced II Corinthians 4:1 and 7, 15-18--"Therefore seeing we have this ministry, as we have received mercy, we faint not; "But we have this treasure in earthen vessels, that the excellency of the power may be of God, and not of us. "For all things are for your sakes, that the abundant grace might through the thanksgiving of many redound to the glory of God. "For which cause we faint not; but though our outward man perish, yet the inward man is renewed day by day. "For our light affliction, which is but for a moment, worketh for us a far more exceeding and eternal weight of glory; "While we look not at the things which are seen, but at the things which are not seen: for the things which are seen are temporal; but the things which are not seen are eternal."

He said earnestly, "Dear people, often when you're doing the best you know how, and you still are experiencing trials, that means you are being faithful to God. It's important to sit down and read your Bible, pray and make sure you aren't being chastened for sin in your life. Also take into consideration how God orchestrated events in your life when you were praying and fasting and the peace He gave you. Don't second-guess those decisions even if your life crumbled afterwards. Instead focus on the good that has come about...even if you have to search for it.

"Remember, Brothers and Sisters, that 'ye serve the Lord Christ.' Colossians 3:24 Your goal shouldn't be to please people. Yes, we are commanded to endeavor to 'live peaceably with all men', but that doesn't mean we worry about them and their opinions more than God's. The 'perfect job' is not just a public ministry at church or abroad, but rather all of life becomes a sweet smelling savor unto the Lord. Both the poor and rich can be consecrated to his service. Even a humble housewife, who sweeps a room, when she does it for the Lord, makes the action holy. She's remembering that 'of the Lord ye shall receive the reward of the inheritance.'

"'Fear not, for I am with thee.' You won't be free from every danger, but God's promise says that you are secure. Those of us who have committed our souls to Christ's keeping will find...'your whole spirit and soul and body be preserved blameless unto the coming of our Lord Jesus Christ. Faithful is he that calleth you, who also will do it.'"

Serena realized that she had allowed her weight to sink into the pew. The powerful words from Scripture washed over her in a cleansing wave. Pastor Eclant's sermons were always good, but today's—the last they'd hear--was especially poignant for her. Why was she so concerned over Jim? She had done her part and prayed. God had convicted him and brought him. He could continue to come on his own, and surely someone else who had more time would take him under his wing. All she needed to do now was be still and listen.

What a comfort. Her facial muscles didn't feel as drawn, and she didn't feel tension in her head. There was freedom in the air around her.

Pastor Eclant concluded, "My last point this evening is to relish in the glory of the Lord. We are all unworthy of God's glory since we always have tendencies to glance sideways toward our own honor. We over-estimate our own powers and need to stand out of the way so that God may be exalted. Often, due to hardships that He brings us into, we are made aware of our own frailness. If our lives are always smooth, we will have few opportunities to be emptied of self and under-qualified to behold the majesty of God and His deliverance. How much more precious to see God's wonders in Pacific waves of embarrassment, financial crises, loss of loved ones, and temptation rather than navigation in little creeks.

"We learn of God's power because we realize our own littleness. Thank God if you have been led down a rough road. This course is what is giving you the experience of God's greatness. Ecclesiastes 10:7—'I have seen servants upon horses, and princes walking as servants upon the earth.' Look how the greatest King of all walked the weary path of service as the Servant of servants. Why do we wonder, then, that we followers should be scorned as inferior? Take heart in the fact that the first are last and the last first.

"Eternity will right the injustices of time. Frequently upstarts claim the highest places while the truly noble toil in obscurity. We must not murmur if this should become our own lot. 'There is none righteous, no, not one.' It's a good thing that God sees Jesus' righteousness in those of us who have accepted Him into our hearts.

"Remember Haman who sat in the court with the king while Mordecai sat in the gate. Would you really choose to take the place of a proud rebel over being a despised Christian? Allow Christ to live through you. 'Every one of us shall give account of himself to God.' Sometimes we ask amiss when we pray. We may be praying counter to the spirit that the Lord would have us grow in.

"Elijah asked to die when he had been threatened by Jezebel. He said, 'Now, O LORD, take away my life; for I am not better than my fathers.' God had a better plan. He ended up carrying him to heaven in a chariot of fire--not having him see death at all. We must make sure we pray God's promises in the Bible and long to magnify Christ rather than gratify our own ease. However, if we ask in faith, nothing wavering, if He doesn't answer exactly as we had expected, we shall receive more than an equivalent for it. If not here on the earth, your reward will be in Heaven hearing God say, 'Well done, thou good and faithful servant.'"

Serena cried out to God silently while she played the organ for the invitation. "Please, God, help me." She couldn't see the entire altar where people came forward to pray because of the way the organ was positioned; but when Pastor read the decision cards aloud, she realized that the one profession of faith was Jim's. Her heart leaped joyfully.

"Please come forward as we dismiss and congratulate our new brother in Christ," Pastor encouraged, "and, Miss Serena, will you please come down here, too?"

Carl was already at the altar to be supportive of Jim. Serena quickly joined them.

Pastor Eclant concluded, "Carl and Serena are planning to move back to New York tomorrow. Brother Carl, do you have anything you'd like to say to everybody?" He handed the microphone to him.

Carl swallowed hard and blinked his eyes. After he cleared his throat, he finally said, "We love you all, and we will miss you.   Thank you for everything...and, Pastor, we'll miss your preaching."

Pastor spoke out, "Tell us you're not leaving!"

Serena felt like she was in a dream. She felt numb as she listened, hardly able to believe how unexpectedly life could change.

Carl's last words were, "Please keep praying for us as well as for Brookelle and Joelle."

Pastor closed out the service with prayer and then urged the people to bid them farewell and shake Jim's hand. The Patton family filed by, and Suzanne hugged Serena and sobbed. When she regained her composure, she held out a pastel heart-shaped pillow with exquisite detail that she had quilted then embellished with a bow of several glossy ribbons at the top. "I hope you'll never forget me."

"Never," Serena assured her as she reached out to touch the girl's silky hair that shone under the lights. "I'll keep on praying for you." Her own eyes were brimming with tears as she watched her follow her family. Looking over at Jim, she saw how bright his blue eyes were. They reflected his newness in Christ where despondency had been before.

Stephen reached him then. "Congratulations!" she heard him say. "You'll never regret your decision. I asked Jesus into my heart when I was ten, and I'm so glad I did. I'll probably see you tomorrow since I'm helping Carl load the truck."

"Most definitely!" Jim agreed. "I'm an excellent packer, and I want everyone to feel free to use my apartment during the move."

By the time she turned the organ off and had straightened the music books, the sanctuary was almost empty. It felt lonely to leave the church for the last time, yet it felt right. They needed to be with their girls.

When Carl parked on their dirty, snow slushy street, Serena was surprised how, over time, this old apartment had begun to feel like home. First thing, she had sprayed, soaked and scoured the tub, toilet and sink. She hadn't showered until the bathroom was safe from germs. Little by little, she had used her Saturday afternoons at home to thoroughly clean. She had vacuumed and scrubbed the floors with carpet stain remover, a scrub brush and an old towel.

Then she had filled their brittle bucket, which had cracks all around the rim, with hot water and pine-scented cleaner. How she'd wished for two more buckets to clean sanitarily. She liked to use one for the soapy wash water, one to squeeze the dirty water from the mop into, and the last to use for rinse water. She had to make do—like normal. At least it had saved time with the one-bucket limitation, and the walls were shinier.

Carl had already taken the futon frame apart, so Serena climbed onto the mattress on the floor with her Bible. She opened it to II Corinthians One. She started reading at verse two where Jerusha had said. "Grace be to you and peace from God our Father, and from the Lord Jesus Christ. Blessed be God, even the Father of our Lord Jesus Christ, the Father of mercies, and the God of all comfort; Who comforteth us in all our tribulation, that we may be able to comfort them which are in any trouble, by the comfort wherewith we ourselves are comforted of God.

"For as the sufferings of Christ abound in us, so our consolation also aboundeth by Christ. And whether we be afflicted, it is for your consolation and salvation, which is effectual in the enduring of the same sufferings which we also suffer: or whether we be comforted, it is for your consolation and salvation. And our hope of you is steadfast, knowing, that as ye are partakers of the sufferings, so shall ye be also of the consolation."

Thursday morning, bright and early, the landlord came to inspect the apartment before he'd return their security deposit. He was an older man who was also involved in several other businesses. Sometimes he called Serena and asked her to go to the newspaper office and look up old articles for him. He reduced fifteen dollars off their rent whenever that happened to repay her for her trouble. Serena couldn't figure how he knew she'd be responsible more than any other tenant. Why would he concern himself with asking her to do business for him? She had only met him once...the day Carl signed the first month's contract.

He came up into the apartment without delay. His scrutinizing eyes seemed to take in every detail. Carl had stacked their boxes neatly against one wall and had taken the table apart. It, along with the futon's pieces and the bag with all the screws, were piled in a corner. Serena had cleaned thoroughly the night before. She felt confident that he'd willingly refund the next month's rent.

The last thing he did was to look in each windowsill. He straightened up authoritatively. "I'll be glad to give you the money once you scrub the mold around the window panes."

Serena took a deep, silent breath. Who did

this man think he was anyway? She had this place much, much cleaner than she had found it upon moving in. Now she understood it all. He was business savvy to the point of using others. He drew her out of her musings.

"I have something to attend to at another of my properties a few blocks over. I'll be back in half an hour. Then I'll pay you. A toothbrush and bleach should do the job nicely." He hurried spryly toward the enclosed staircase.

Serena stared at Carl in disgust. "I don't have any bleach, and I really don't want to paw through boxes to find an old brush," she whispered in despair.

"I'm so sorry, Honey. I can't believe it. He just knows you'll do it. He must figure he may as well get all he can out of this deal. I'll run down to the store, and I'll help you."

"Thank you, Honey, but shouldn't I go in case some of the men arrive soon?"

"Good thinking," Carl agreed. "You know, Serena, God may be using this act of servitude to put Christian actions behind our words since we sent him an evangelistic Christmas card with our month's rent."

Serena nodded. "You're right. I'll try to have a better attitude."

When Mr. Hatt returned, he was pleased. "It's been nice doing business with you," he said simply. He handed Carl the check and asked Serena if she'd mind doing more research for him in the future.

"No." Serena's response was absolute. "Thank you, Mr. Hatt, but we'll be living out of state." She shook his outstretched hand politely. Then Carl took his turn.

The man didn't hesitate. "I have another appointment momentarily. Good day to you both."

Jim was the first man to arrive early. Carl invited him up and offered him a doughnut. "Thanks," he said. "They look great, but I'll wait to have one after I've worked off my breakfast."

Carl grinned. "All right. I'm ready to start."

The men made a good team and had made good progress by the time Stephen and the other two church members arrived. Before long, Mr. Shelby came up the steps with a yellow card envelope in hand. "Good morning, Miss Serena. How are you doing?" he asked sincerely. His eyes were empathetic.

Serena smiled. "I'm doing great! Just to know that I'll be with my girls soon is almost all I can think about."

He nodded. "Please," he said, handing her the cheery envelope, "take this from me and my wife. Promise me you won't open it, though, until you're traveling."

"Yes, Sir," Serena agreed. She looked at him gratefully. "We really appreciate your offer to bury Allegra beside your first wife. You will always have a special place in our hearts."

By the time the men had carried out the last box, the last two movers showed up. Jim announced, "Please, everybody, feel free to use my apartment if you need the facilities. Some coffee is brewed. Serena has doughnuts, and I made sandwiches this morning that are wrapped and labeled if you'd like to grab a few to eat over at the storage unit."

Serena walked down with Carl. Jim was a surprisingly neat housekeeper. She was sure some of the contribution was the fact that he was a bachelor. Men didn't seem to collect as much décor. All of his necessities were in place; and the residence sported a sparse, clutter-free environment. He did have a few pictures of snowy mountain slopes hanging on the walls, and Serena felt at home.

While they ate the doughnuts, Jim talked. "Reading of your losing Allegra reminded me of my wife. Jeannie and I married when we were both twenty. She was an exceptional caterer. She provided the food for many of the Daytonian elites' parties. She could arrange the tables to look like extravagant gardens, and all the 'flowers' would be made with edible items.

"She rented a community industrial kitchen and could follow any wholesome theme the hosts or hostesses would request. She would color her cookie dough and cut it and ice and adorn each baked cookie with other baked shapes until they were fantastically realistic. I'm not just prejudice either. Her food was tasty. I learned how to cook from her.

"She poured her heart into the work, trying to distract herself from the fact that she was physically unable to have children. We devised a goal to work toward. We both began to save our earnings. After two years of scrimping with little fun, we were ready to look at houses. We looked with our realtor, over the course of several months, until we found the perfect house. It had room enough for several children that we hoped to adopt. It was closer to the neighborhoods Jeannie catered in and to my office.

"The housing track was older but very distinguished. Mature trees lined the streets, and each home seemed to be lovingly cared for. The elderly woman that had lived in the house for twenty-five years had maintained it beautifully. We would just have to update the seventies' décor as we came up with the money. The thing we really liked about the place was that it was situated at the end of a cul-de-sac. There wouldn't be any through traffic, and the yard backed up to a well-known golf course that wouldn't be in jeopardy of being developed into more housing plats. Jeannie loved the spacious floor plan, and we'd have public sewer and water to avoid country problems.

"Our offer was accepted the following day, and we decided that we had earned a celebration. We hadn't been out to eat in what seemed like ages. On our way to a Chinese restaurant, we discussed color schemes we'd like for each room. At the last minute, we decided to turn into a home improvement store. We still had a yellow arrow as I whipped into the left lane. Just as I turned into the oncoming lane, an SUV ran a red light. Jeannie was killed instantly. I couldn't bear to move without her, so I backed out of the contract.

"With all the money we had saved, along with her life policy, I've been living like a bum for a year. I still work, but I cared little about anything else. I even began smoking for the first time. Nothing eased my pain like I had hoped. My sister in-law has tried to win me to Christ, but I always refused. When I read your paper about how you lost your little girl, I respected your cheerfulness and hard work ethics more than ever."

Chapter Thirteen

Reuniting

    Serena followed the moving truck in the station wagon and watched the familiar territory pass by. She and Carl had spent years in Ohio. Would they ever return? The circumstances had fallen into place so quickly. The sun was shining brightly, and the roads were dry. Serena willed Carl to drive a little faster. She could barely wait to hug their girls tightly and never let them go again.

    She glanced down at the seat. The card from Mr. Shelby was safe beside her. Whenever they passed a rest area sign, Serena hoped that Carl wouldn't stop. She was eager to be there already. Once they were past Cleveland, the weather suddenly changed. The sun was blotted out, and snow was heavy in the air. Serena released the gas pedal and strained to see Carl's taillights come on. She turned her lights on as the car slowed. Still she couldn't make out the truck in front of her.

Then she caught a glimpse of him. He had his four ways on, so she followed suit. She prayed that no careless driver would fly up behind and smash into her. After creeping along in the blizzard, the snow eased some...just enough for them to see cars and trucks in the median and off the sides of the highway. She and Carl were accustomed to winter driving, having grown up in New York. Serena figured that the out of state drivers from farther away were having a more difficult time compensating and allowing the steering wheels to right themselves occasionally.

It felt like hours of driving in the scouring, blinding snow when Carl led the way onto an exit ramp. They parked side by side in the rest area's parking lot, and they both jumped out to meet each other. Snow salted Carl's dark hair turning it white. Serena felt the fluffy flakes settle on her eyelashes and saw them melt into droplets as she listened to Carl. "Do you still want to keep going, or would you rather stop at a hotel for the night?"

Serena didn't hesitate. "Please, may we continue on as we have been?" She felt an impatience that was growing more difficult to contain. She felt like she did when she had been expecting her girls. The closer she had come to reaching her due dates, the farther away they had seemed.

Carl sighed in relief. "I was hoping you'd feel the same way. Let's lock up the vehicles and stretch before we get going again."

When they returned from the rest rooms, and he opened the car door for her to climb back in, she held up the card. "Carl, please come in with me for a minute." She slid over to make room, and he shut the door behind them. After she slid her finger under the flap, she handed it to Carl. "It's from Mr. Shelby."

The entire cover was a big, droopy-eyed dogface with a bubble that read, *You're really going?* When Carl opened it, several bills floated down into his lap. He made sure that none fell on the floor before continuing to read. *It's difficult to say good-bye, but it helps to know that God will be watching over you. We will miss you more than you know. You've come through so many things; and, each time, you've allowed the Lord to make you sweeter. As you face this new phase of your lives, be assured that our Saviour will guide you, and you're on the winning side. Matthew 11:28— "Come unto Me, all ye that labor and are heavy laden, and I will give you rest."*

Mr. Shelby had written personally, My wife and I believe that God has some very special service for you because your love for the Lord shines from your hearts. Thank you for your yielded lives. We hope this money helps the rocks in the road to become stepping-stones in your journey. You've demonstrated your gratefulness over and over for Allegra's cemetery plot by also beautifully maintaining my first wife's. Be assured that we will do the same for your precious daughter's now that you'll be gone. Whenever we go there, we'll be reminded of you and will pray for you. You've become like daughter and son to us. Please don't ever hesitate to call us or to request something specific you'd like for us to put on Allegra's grave, free of charge.

Lovingly,
Mr. and Mrs. Shelby

P.S.—We wanted to give you cash rather than a check in case you needed it on your trip or for your first month's rent without having to get to a bank.

Carl looked at Serena. Tears were streaming down his face, and Serena just stared back at him. Carl grasped the money and handed it to her. "I won't be able to see to count it."

"I feel overwhelmed yet greedy," she said as she began counting. She set it firmly on his leg when she finished. "No wonder he reminded me to keep the card safely in my care before he headed home. This is sure enough for one month's rent."

"How much?" Carl asked impatiently, brushing at his eyes with his hands.

"One *thousand* dollars!"

"More than enough," Carl exhaled. "Parting can sure be sweet sorrow because you find out who your true friends are. Do you see God's hand on this move so far?"

"I do."

Carl reached for her hand and thanked God for Mr. and Mrs. Shelby's encouraging words and their sacrificial gift. He asked God to bless them in return and for protection on the roads. He split the money and handed Serena half. Tuck some in each of your boots. I'll do the same. It makes me nervous to carry this much money, but we'll do our part to be wise. God will take care of the rest."

Once they passed through Pennsylvania and farther from Lake Erie, the snow eased some; but the roads were still treacherous. Once, despite going only forty miles an hour, Serena hit an icy spot and began spinning. She didn't hit the brake until the wheels seemed to grip into some thicker snow. She slowly pumped it and came to a complete stop. She sat shaking as she faced oncoming traffic. Quickly, she took her foot off the brake and turned the wheel as she eased her foot onto the gas pedal again. "Please, God, help me to get going!" The tires began to spin before suddenly getting traction, and the car jerked forward.

Carl had pulled off to the side down a stretch, but Serena knew she didn't have time to move over behind him without slipping again. A tractor-trailer was gaining on her, and there were two cars in the passing lane. They couldn't slow down without hitting the icy patch themselves, so she urged the gas pedal closer to the floor. Serena didn't dare look in her rear view mirror. She stared straight ahead, concentrating on driving, but expecting a jolt any moment.

The cars passed her. The sound of the tractor's huge tires grinding into the snow and the whirring filled Serena's ears. Then it was ahead of her. She was safe. Her body felt icy and numb as the pulsating adrenalin began to subside. Carl kept a distance behind her the rest of the way home allowing her to set the pace that felt safest to her. Serena knew that he hoped to take the brunt of the crash from the traffic if she should lose control again.

The stretch of highway from Salamanca to Horseheads always seemed endless. It was so much later than Serena's parents had expected them. She figured that the girls would already be asleep and that supper would be long past. She flipped on the radio, and the hymn about love lifting her was playing. She thought about how true those words were. She served a mighty God that would give His own life for her, comfort her with the Holy Spirit, and even bless her with friends that put their love into action for her and Carl.

Finally, they turned into her parents' driveway at three a.m. The house looked like a Christmas tree. Every inside and outside light seemed to be on. She relished in the still, solid ground beneath her feet as she stiffly clambered out. Before Carl had landed beside her on the shoveled pavement, the back door flew open, and everyone rushed out joyfully calling their names. "Mommy, Daddy!!" "Carl and Serena!" Then they were in each other's arms.

"We kept coming out and shoveling with Grandpa!" Joelle bragged.

"We helped Grandma set the table a long time ago, but supper won't take long," Brookelle added.

Serena smiled and sobbed in turn. She and Carl passed the girls back and forth, squeezing them and caressing their soft faces as they studied the changes several months had made. Mom took Serena's arm and led her toward the house. Dad followed Carl. "We don't want you catching cold your first night home."

As soon as they opened the door, Serena smelled Mom's homemade French fries and onions as the warm air wafted over them. Mom kept saying, "It's so wonderful to have you both here." Dad smiled from ear to ear and patted Carl firmly on the back.

Serena knelt down on the tile and drew both girls against her, breathing in the lavender scent of their freshly washed hair. "Now I can talk to *you*. I won't have to replay your messages on the answering machine. I can hardly wait to see your souvenirs from your trip to Lancaster."

Dad had disappeared then returned from the deck with freshly grilled, marinated chicken breasts. "I knew these are your favorite, Carl; so Mom let me do the meat for the meal."

"Mmmm!" Carl moaned appreciatively, rubbing his stomach and smiling.

"We ladies made cherry pie, Mommy, since it's your favorite," Brookelle informed her happily.

After everyone had eaten their fill, they savored the dessert along with hot chocolate. Then the twins curled up contentedly, each pillowing a head in Carl's and Serena's laps. They were soon breathing slowly and peacefully. Serena stroked Brookelle's silky hair, and the glint from the flames in the gas fireplace made it glisten.

Serena broke the silence. "Dad and Mom, we can't thank you both enough. We could only make it through knowing that you were here lovingly teaching the girls the way you did me. I was able to pour myself into my job. Claire and Blaire...the entire Huff family, as well as the housekeeper and her husband, became my mission field. Allegra had prayed and asked forgiveness for her sins and Jesus into her heart. I knew that she was safe in Heaven where Satan could never harm her again, and Joelle and Brookelle were having Bible time with you as well as attending church."

"I know Serena gave her charges as good an education as she'd give our own girls," Carl praised. "I don't think that family knew what they had in Serena." Then he choked up, his shoulders shaking, as he tried to thank them, too.

Dad knelt beside him and hugged him. "We love you, Carl," Dad assured him.

Mom stood up. "Something came in the mail for you, Serena. It came yesterday...actually the day before, now that it's morning. Let me get it."

Soon she was back with the business envelope in hand. "Here it is."

Serena took it curiously. "Thank you, Mom. I can't imagine what..." Then she saw the return address label. *Pianoforte* and *New York, NY caught* her attention. "The contest that Stephen Eclant had given me paperwork for." Nervously, she pulled out the contents. She skimmed the first few lines. "I've been accepted." She looked at Carl apprehensively. "We just got here, and I don't want to leave already."

Carl rubbed her back encouragingly. "Honey, you've barely read the letter. Remember how we've prayed for God to open doors as He sees fit? It's late, and we need to get to bed. A fresh morning always makes things look better."

"You're right, of course."

Dad yawned, and Mom stifled one.

"That sounds like a good idea," Dad affirmed. He stood up and stretched.

Mom said, "I'll show you which bed is which girl's, and you may lay them down just like that if you think it's okay. I make sure they brush their teeth twice a day. Missing one time in months is pretty good, I'd say. The girls were thrilled to put on their pajamas in the evening and to know that they were going to stay up. They said, 'It will be like a slumber party!'"

Once Carl and Serena had carried the girls in and tucked the blankets around them, Mom showed them Dad's office where she had rolled out a foam rubber mattress and made it up for them. "Is there anything you'll need since you haven't unloaded yet?"

"I think we're set," Serena assured her. "Just to lie down and sleep will be heavenly."

Carl gave her a big bear hug first. "Mom, thank you a million times from the bottom of our hearts."

Mom wiped at a tear. "Isn't that what parents are for...to be there for their children and grandchildren? Now we'll rest secure knowing that your family is together again. The girls were wonderful, but you'll never know how much they pined for you both."

After Dad and Mom had finished in the bathroom and shut their bedroom door, Carl and Serena tiptoed back into the girls' room. They knelt down and watched them sleep for a few minutes. Carl quietly prayed aloud, thanking God. Serena could hardly bear to leave them to go to bed.

After sleeping for three delightful hours, Carl stirred at the sound of the alarm on his watch. "I need to head over to the storage unit and start unloading before I miss today's deadline for turning the truck back in and end up paying for an extra day."

He staggered up sleepily and opened the door. Serena forced the warm blankets back and stumbled off the mattress, too. It would be another full day, but it'd have their girls in it. That was what mattered most.

God continued to confirm their move as He orchestrated the events of the day as only He could. Feeling compelled to look through the phone book while he ate a quick bowl of cereal, Carl decided to call different machine shops. Being a Friday, it was amazing when his second call afforded him an impromptu interview that very morning. He shaved, showered and left.

The owner of the small carbide tool shop hired him on the spot and even referred him to a realtor he trusted that could help them find a rental. Her office was just a block away from the shop, so Carl drove there directly. She gladly handed him a stack of print-outs in their price range to take home to look over with Serena before they both returned to walk through some of the apartments with her later that afternoon.

The girls were eager to join them, and Carl and Serena were thrilled to have them. Their exuberance made the day seem like an adventure. Before they met the realtor, they drove by the ten places. They ruled out six of them by their looks or location.   Then when they toured the four hopefuls with Jennifer, one in particular seemed like home. The pleasant real estate agent just laughed in disbelief when they told her that they were ready with a cash deposit in hand and the landlord agreed to their moving in that evening. Carl didn't mind paying for an extra day for the moving truck since they'd be saving a lot of money by not needing a storage unit...thanks to Mr. Shelby.

Carl's trip to work each morning would be highway driving, too. Although it was just a rental property, Serena felt she would be content to stay here indefinitely. There was peace of mind knowing that anything that may need repair would be seen to by the owner without their going farther into debt.

Dad, Mr. Ingersoll—his neighbor, and two men from their church helped Carl make quick work of unloading since their few belongings were meager. "Packing always takes longer," Carl cheerfully admitted to the men, relieved that the dreaded job was over. "Thanks, Guys!"

Chapter Fourteen

New York City

    Serena clambered onto the bus as fast as she could before Joelle or Brookelle could ask her one more question. Tears had already filled her eyes, and they would spill over onto her cold cheeks if she had to look into their pleading eyes one more time. The same words they had repeated all morning kept haunting her. "Please don't leave, Mommy." Carl smiled bravely for her sake.

    They had prayed for a month about the Grand Pianoforte Conservatory Contest and the yearlong performance tour contract if she placed. They mutually decided that they should be willing to sacrifice for twelve more months to further increase their financial status. They were resolved never to have their girls apart from them again and wanted to prepare for unexpected crises. At least this way, Carl would be with them. Serena would be in and out every other weekend that was better than being apart indefinitely like they had been in Ohio. Serena's mom offered to watch the girls while Carl was at work, and Serena felt less apologetic since Carl agreed to home school them in the evenings.

She found an empty seat close to the front and slid in against the tinted window. Carl was between the girls holding their mittened hands. Their breath steamed into the air, and tears glistened icily on their eyelashes. Serena's mom and dad had taken them all out to eat at an Italian restaurant the night before. Mom had said, "You'll need time alone and privacy at the station tomorrow. You've been family-deprived for so long. Just know that you will be in our hearts and minds all morning." Dad's gentle blue eyes had reassured her of his love before she hugged him. He was slow to release her; and when he did, he managed a wobbly smile.

Serena waved through the window at her little family, but they couldn't see her. A steady line of people in snow boots clomped up the two steps and scuffed down the rubbery aisle. A gray-haired woman sat down beside her as the driver pushed the handle that pulled the long lever, shutting the door. She bumped into Serena but didn't apologize or move closer to the aisle. Making herself comfortable, she set two large carry-on bags between their feet and removed her bulky coat.

There was a stale odor that permeated the air space, and Serena felt trapped. She smiled politely at the passenger but tried to keep her face toward the cool glass. The woman began to talk, and Serena could feel her watching her. Reluctantly she turned around. This stranger had relentless eye contact and never seemed to stop for breath.

As the large bus began to move, Serena panicked for a last glimpse of her family and rudely turned her back to look. They all looked so forlorn. Would they stop for lunch before driving the hour and a half back home? Carl would not let her ride the short transit from Elmira to Binghamton. He didn't want her switching buses without him. He didn't like the idea, either, of her finding a taxi once she reached New York City. Serena had tried to reassure him that God would protect her and that once she was in the taxi, her next destination would be the conservatory. There was no way she'd go exploring into the subway tunnels even if the trains were faster.

The woman cleared her throat conspicuously. For two hours, Serena breathed through her mouth so she wouldn't smell. She got a kink in her neck listening to her ramble on and on about insignificant happenings and memories. Would she ever stop talking? By the time they'd arrive in New York, she'd be in desperate need of her asthma inhaler. This woman must have had a cat or dog or was wearing a dusty coat. A pang of conscience jarred her to the realization that she had been neglecting the opportunity to represent Christ.

She didn't know this person. Surely by this age, she had endured several hardships that were unseen to passersby. She was acting the very way she hated others to treat her. This repulsiveness she was inclined to have toward the woman was only inward haughtiness because she subconsciously felt that she was better. *What a spiritual malignancy,* she silently scolded herself. *Here you are bitter toward others for not treating you better and, in turn, becoming the very characteristic you despise. Maybe God is trying to humble you by reminding you not to respect the proud.*

For the next three hours, Serena tried her best to gladly listen. She actually began to find the lady interesting despite the embarrassing wheezing sound that her lungs made when she breathed. She tried to inhale shallowly so that it wouldn't be noticeable. Then the driver spoke into his microphone; "We are half an hour from the city, Folks. Thank you for choosing our line for your traveling needs. Should you need any assistance upon our arrival, there will be an employee standing outside the door when we pull up. Please remain seated until I dismiss you. It's been a pleasure to serve you."

Serena took advantage of the interruption to ask, "Ma'am, my name is Serena. What is yours?"

"Corliss," she said in surprise.

"*Mrs.* Corliss?"

"No, no. Corliss is my first name, which is Old English for good-hearted and joyful. My husband, Mr. Armstrong, grew vineyards along Seneca Lake. What beautiful scenery I've enjoyed for our entire marriage, but he died five years ago. My daughter finally convinced me to come to live with her. I'm not fond of cities myself, but the loneliness finally got to me. I found a buyer I trusted to take over my husband's business without putting a 'for sale' sign out. I've really enjoyed talking with you, young lady. You don't seem two-faced. I sense true compassion in you."

"Thank you, Mrs. Armstrong, but it's only because you see Jesus in me. I really am sorry about your husband, though." Serena didn't dare ask about his death until she finished, or she'd never get another chance to talk. She pulled out a tract that she had placed in her pocket that morning. "I asked Jesus into my heart when I was four, and I have never regretted that decision once. He's there for me when those I love can't be. This paper will tell you what the Bible says about Heaven and Hell and how I was saved from my sin. It's yours to keep. Please read it as soon as you get a moment. We don't know when it will be our time to die. My daughter Allegra died suddenly when she was only eight. If you don't mind my asking, how did your husband die?"

Serena welcomed the cold air when she stepped off the bus. The station was many times the size of the one in Binghamton. There were so many signs with directional arrows and people bustling about that she felt completely disoriented. A young man had reached the assistant first, so Serena was waiting in line when Corliss approached her. "Serena, this is my daughter Candace. She came to pick me up. We can give you a lift if your destination isn't too far away."

"Hello, Candace." Serena shook her hand firmly. "How nice of you, but I promised my husband that I'd ride in a taxi. Who would have thought kind people like you would offer such a thing? I would appreciate your help, though, in pointing me in the right direction."

The young woman was as beautiful as a news reporter. Her brown eyes looked at Serena curiously then her lips curved to reveal a sparkly white and even smile.   "No problem at all." Serena wondered why her mother wasn't as groomed. As they parted, Candace advised, "A word of caution, Serena…try not to look like a tourist by staring up at the tall buildings, and be sure to hold your purse in front of you. I hope you enjoy your stay in the city."

By the time Serena locked herself in the dormitory room, she was exhausted from her struggle to breathe. She didn't like to use the inhaler in front of people and have them think that she was doing it to get attention. Sitting down on the bed, she unzipped her purse and pulled the medication out. She shook it while she exhaled as long as she could. Then she sealed her lips around the mouthpiece and plugged her nose before pushing the pump that metered the mist of aerosol. She inhaled slowly and deeply before breathing back out. She repeated the order one more time.

Then she knelt down beside the single bed. "Dear Lord," she cried out, "this situation is foreign to me. Please protect me as I'm alone with no protection in this big building and only a few people in other rooms. I even have to share a bathroom that's out in the hallway, and You know what germs could be there. This type of job can obviously be lonesome behind the scenes. Thank You for giving me the opportunity to spend time with You and for the safe trip here."

She decided to call Carl before she read her Bible, so he wouldn't be worried. She had left the phone off during the trip. It gave her a secure feeling just to have it with her. Carl answered, and the girls were laughing in the background. "Hi, Honey," he said with relief in his voice. "We've been stopping to pray for you throughout the day. Are you safe in your room for the night?"

"Yes, Carl, only it isn't a hotel like we thought. I'm in a dormitory and even have to share a bathroom. It's a stately older stone building, and there are lots of lights in the hallways. Thankfully I don't have to share my room with anyone. Still, I'd much rather be with you. I miss you and the girls already. Our four weeks together were like a dream; the time was so short lived."

"I know," Carl agreed, somehow seeming distracted. "How was your trip?"

"It was difficult because I didn't want to use the bathroom. It would have been embarrassing to ask Mrs. Armstrong to stand up for me to get out then to walk past so many passengers. I still had to wait until my taxi ride was over. The thing is, I haven't drunk much at all today on purpose. I still feel a frequency...probably due to being all keyed up about tomorrow. If I need to use the restroom during the night, I'm planning on holding it and not going until it's morning."

"You feel free to call me anytime if you are frightened or need to go. Okay?" he said earnestly.

"Thank you, Honey. That's reassuring. How did your day go with the girls?"

"Fine. The girls were a wreck as your bus left, so for a distraction we stopped for fast food. We shared fries and chicken nuggets. When we got home, we bundled up and made a snow fort. Then we had some hot chocolate. I started to read them a story, but we all fell asleep on the floor. Then..." The girls squealed loudly, and Carl paused. "I love you, Serena. I'm sure you'll do great tomorrow night."

"Love you, too! Give the girls kisses for me, and thanks for praying."

She pressed the end button then set the cell phone on the nightstand. Feeling too vulnerable to change, she slipped off her shoes, pulled back the covers and slid her cold feet under the sheet. "Hot chocolate sure sounds good right now," she groaned to herself. She propped the flat pillows behind her the best she could and tucked up her knees. Setting her Bible on them, she read a few chapters.

A slamming door startled Serena. The clock read six a.m. She hadn't expected to sleep, especially sitting up. Her neck was stiffer than it had been after the bus ride, but she was safe...and today was the competition! "Thank You, God," she praised. Serena tidied up the room and brushed and sprayed her hair. She'd shower this afternoon...shared bathroom or not. Surely the other contestants would be showering this morning and waiting their turns. Looking under the bed and all around, she made sure she wasn't leaving anything behind. She'd carry her duffel bag with her until she found the lockers. She *had* to use the bathroom right now. After unlocking and opening the door, she peered out to see if it was vacant. The door was shut, and light shown out from under it.

Popping some freshening gum into her mouth, Serena followed the building's layout map and hurried down the halls and winding staircases toward the entrance foyer. She heard other accomplished pianists' muffled practicing already as she passed by closed doors near the front desk. Excitement began to mount again now that it was daytime.

Suddenly, a wave of nausea washed over her. Her lips felt cold, and she was dizzy. She needed to find a bathroom—fast! Hoping she had enough time to ask the young man behind the desk, she hurried over. "Sir?" she managed, swallowing hard. Then she spotted a varnished sign hanging from a bracket and ran toward it. She made it through the door and into a stall just in time. This wasn't the time to get sick.

When she returned to the foyer, she eased into a plush, wide chair. Large, arched windows allowed daylight to flood the area. It wasn't sunny, but at least it wasn't dismal gray either. She felt safer near the main entrance and the secretary. She pawed through her purse until she found the package of chocolate-covered peanuts Carl had bought for her before the trip. She tore it open and shook a few into her palm. After she chewed the handful, she took several deep breaths. It was a good thing Mrs. Armstrong had distracted her and she never ate them on the bus.

When she trusted her legs to carry her, she approached the desk. "I'm sorry about earlier. May I have a schedule for the day, please?"

"Have you filled out all the necessary paperwork?" the man asked, pulling a schedule from a wooden organizer on the desk.

"Yes. I did that yesterday when I arrived."

"Your name, please?" the man asked.

"Serena Callahan."

"The secretary yesterday overlooked your contract information," he said, handing her some stapled papers along with the schedule. "It would be a good idea to read it thoroughly before this evening. Some of the clauses in it have been changed from the sample form that was mailed to you in the pre-registration packet, and you must be prepared to sign it if you place tonight. Also, there is a continental breakfast being served in the cafeteria." Then, nodding toward the hallway, he said, "Whenever you're ready, I'll give you a key to a piano room for practice."

"Thank you."

Serena found the cafeteria without any problems, but she didn't think she could stomach cold cereal. She craved scrambled eggs with melted cheddar cheese; but since they weren't offered, she decided upon a bagel with butter and a large glass of orange juice. She found a table near a front window and prayed. While she ate, she read the updated contract. One clause in particular seemed to jump out at her.

"No pregnancies allowed due to the frequent traveling and for the sake of appearance. Any other health conditions must be disclosed to the board for consideration at the time of the signing. Should you be disqualified from the traveling position for such a reason, you will be bound for the same amount of time to teach piano lessons to aspiring musicians or your place will be awarded to the next runner up. Your salary will be discussed at the time of the final agreement; and your accommodations will be provided, free of charge, in the dormitory."

How could this be? She and Carl had been holding off to have another child until they were more stable monetarily, but she couldn't guarantee that something wouldn't happen. She couldn't possibly bear living apart from her family in this building for a year. Traveling and being in safer hotel rooms was one thing, but this scenario was completely different.

She had come too far to back out of the competition. What could she do? There was no way she'd purposely make mistakes tonight to try to lose. That would be a poor testimony as well as humbling. She forced herself to finish most of the food and swallowed the last of the cold juice before returning to the dormitory foyer.

She felt dazed as she asked for a key. Shutting the door behind her, she leaned against it and slid down. She sat there on the floor asking God. "Why does every circumstance for our family have to be complicated, Lord? Please take care of this predicament for me. I don't want this job if I'll be forced to be on birth control or possibly be a prisoner of sorts here in the city."

She hadn't read her Bible yet that morning. Now that her stomach felt better, she could concentrate. She pulled it from her bag. The Scriptures reassured her as much as if she were safe in Carl's embrace. "In quietness and in confidence shall be your strength...blessed are all they that wait for him...he will be very gracious unto you, and therefore will he be exalted, that he may have mercy upon you: for the LORD is a God of judgment: blessed are all they that wait for him. Ye shall have a song, and gladness of heart..."

On a large sticky note beside the passage, she had taken notes from a missionary who had preached in Ohio. He had preached about the star that the shepherds saw when Jesus was born. Reminding the congregation about stars being humanly innumerable, he emphasized the important role that one specific star played.

She had written: Be passionate about the task God has assigned to you. The star wasn't seeking fame. You can tell by what the wise men said to King Herod. "Where is he that is born King of the Jews? for we have seen his star in the east, and are come to worship him." Do we cause others to be drawn to Jesus Christ? There are so many different colored lights at Christmas time...red, green, blue, and yellow. Some even flash. Always remember the white star representing purity. Are we willing to declare that we seek a better country, that of Heaven? Psalm 21:6b says, "Thou hast made him exceeding glad with thy countenance." Do we have a glow about us that makes people wonder what's different about us? Our examples will shine brighter if our flames continue to burn when we're put to the test.

Carl had encouraged her to compete, so she would do her best and not doubt since her motives were to ultimately better their family life.   She could trust God to work everything out.   She must.

Early that afternoon, after having practiced for several hours to feel limbered up and eating a meat and lettuce sandwich in the busy cafeteria, she headed for the dorm floor to shower. As she began climbing the stairs, Corliss's daughter Candace was coming down.   Serena smiled and greeted her.

"Why, hello!" the woman exclaimed familiarly...almost sounding like a question. "May I help you?" Her dark eyes mirrored her apparent, *What are you doing here?*

"I am competing in the Grand Pianoforte Contest this evening, and I need to freshen up."

"Oh, yes. Of course. Were you planning to use one of the dorm's bathrooms?"

Serena nodded.

"If you'll follow me, I'll show you to a much nicer one that the contestants wouldn't know about."

"Thank you!" Serena agreed with feeling. "I wasn't exactly glad to use the other. I take it that you work here?"

"Yes. I am a theory instructor and stage manager on days like today." She patted Serena's shoulder in a friendly manner. As their heels clicked down the marble-floored hallway, Candace thanked her for showing an interest in her mother on the bus trip.

"Mother has been in a world of her own for years. Since Dad's love was the vineyards, they'd work outside together for hours each day. Mom was terribly worried, after he died, that she'd fail his business. So she worked even harder to make up for his absence. She began to neglect her house first--which eventually led to her personal hygiene as well. All her efforts were poured into the vineyards.

"Mom was always extremely conscientious about her grooming before. I was shocked the first time I visited her several months after the funeral. She had become a recluse and never had any fun. It sure took a lot of convincing to get her to come here. Let me tell you."

Candace chuckled in her femininely low voice and politely chewed her gum. Serena could smell that it was cinnamon...her favorite. Today, however, it made her feel more nauseous.

"Anyway," Candace continued, "she had been dreading the trip; but when she arrived, she was bustling about--all concerned over you. It's wonderful to see a glimpse of her old self. I want you to know how much I appreciate your listening to my mom. A lot must get bottled up when a person lives alone and doesn't mingle with others." She held out her hand as a pointing gesture.

Serena stopped and looked. "We are backstage!"

Candace seemed pleased. "I thought you might enjoy a sneak preview." Taking her arm, she led her through the curtains. She flipped on a stage light and stood still, releasing her. The rich black piano shone as glossy as it possibly could.

Serena couldn't contain herself but glided across the floor. She caught herself just before touching it, not wanting to smudge the finish. Looking back at Candace, she asked, "May I lift the lid?"

Candace bent her head in assent before Serena secured her fingertips beneath the lip and slowly lifted it. A long strip of red felt had been rolled over the keyboard in an elegant display of care. She stared breathlessly at the eighty-eight white and black shiny keys that she would be touching soon when she played her selection.

"The piano, and the organ taking a close second, evoke such an inspiring thrill inside me," Serena confessed. "Mom has a picture of me sitting on her piano bench when I was only nine months old. My grin couldn't have been any bigger. I've attended several concerts over the years and enjoyed them immensely, but I never thought I'd actually be performing in one...besides a wedding or a play."

Suddenly snapping out of her reverie, she eased the lid back down. "I've taken enough of your time and should get out of here before I get nervous." She turned her head and scanned the rows of seats and front of the balcony. "It's a good thing the spotlights are nearly blinding. I remember from a play I was in that they felt like a hot barrier, separating me from the crowd and my stage fright."

"Like a security blanket," Candace agreed, sounding like she understood.

Serena nodded.

"Well," Candace said as they went backstage, "The bathroom in this far corner is separate from the dressing room, and only those of us on staff know about it."

"Oh!" Serena exclaimed as she walked in. "It's spacious and elegant! I'll be relieved to have this nearby while I wait my turn tonight. It must be due to my nerves, but I keep running to the restroom. I had to go several times during my practicing today and more than normal yesterday."

Candace eyed her suspiciously. "Are you prone to urinary infections?"

"No," Serena answered honestly.

"Could you be...? Well, you know what I'm implying. Did you read the contract yet?"

"Yes."

"You are?"

"No. I mean, I did look over the contract this morning." Serena suddenly felt tingly from head to foot and conspicuously confused. "My husband and I have been careful not to have another baby yet because we're trying to get back on our feet since our house burned and our daughter died. We had accidentally overlooked mailing out the insurance payment that month, so the coverage had lapsed. All that to say, I have been so busy working to help my husband financially that I hadn't even noticed."

Candace impulsively hugged her and urged, "You need to get ready for this evening and *enjoy* it. There will be plenty of time to discuss this afterwards. I'll be back in an hour after I assist some of the other contestants. Then there's something I'd like to show you before you must stay backstage."

Serena showered then carefully applied her makeup and nail polish while her hair air-dried. Once her fingernails' color was set, she curled her hair. She was spraying it when Candace returned, walking through the open doorway. She slid a paper shopping bag onto the countertop. "This is for you to look in after I bring you back. Come, come!" she urged cheerfully.

They made their way across the stage, through the auditorium and lobby then between the elaborate outside French doors. Serena stared in amazement at the difference of this entrance compared to the one she had come in the previous day. The evening darkness also contributed to the majesty of the building. It was lit with ambient, clean whiteness from the numerous brass lanterns that were cemented on the walls and to the many granite steps that twisted upward toward them. Elegantly dressed trumpeters stood on either side of every five steps playing a majestic song clearly in the crisp air. "They're warming up before the 'early birds' begin to arrive," Candace explained.

Puffs of warm breath exhaled from the trumpets' bells as the men harmoniously blew in synchronism. The scene caused her to think of Heaven as the music surrounded her. The men, all in black tuxedos, seemed oblivious to the ladies' presence as they stared toward the pink glow of the city sky. Every merging note that floated easily into the air, stirred within her the desire to play just as beautifully on the piano tonight. She would offer her talent to God, picturing herself in a bubble on the bench with Jesus, like her teacher used to say. If she could play with her whole heart as if she were in Heaven and do it for His glory alone, she'd be happy.

She shivered involuntarily, and her new friend didn't overlook it. "You need to go inside. We can't have you getting chilled before you play." As they returned to the warmth of the building, Candace said, "Now you know what it will be like for the audience as they begin arriving. Even their entrance prepares them for quality entertainment that they have come to expect."

"Wow!" agreed Serena nodding her head. "That's something. I've never seen anything like it. Thank you...I guess." She laughed. "Maybe I'll be more nervous and need to visit the restroom more than ever. I can make it backstage on my own just fine. You must be a busy lady, and I don't want to steal all your time."

Candace said, "You didn't steal my time, because I offered to show you. I'll see you in the dressing room in a little bit then."

Serena walked down the plush carpet on the steep aisle. If only Carl and the girls could be here, but maybe it was for the best that they weren't. An audience full of strangers wasn't as intimidating as people she knew. She climbed the stage steps; and as she walked behind the curtains and down the hall, she heard voices in the dressing room. Serena hurried by without glancing in, so she wouldn't get stuck talking with anyone until she had seen what was in the bag. She hoped no one had found the bathroom. The bag was still on the countertop, so she quickly shut the door before turning on the light—not wanting to attract attention to the lavatory until she was through.

Picking up the bag as quietly as possible, she carried it to a back corner where there was a padded metal chair with an ornate back and a small round table covered with a lace cloth. The paper sack crinkled as she sat down and opened it. There was a pregnancy test, a protein drink and a card. Serena stared into the bag in stunned amazement. How could this woman be so thoughtful when she hardly knew her...and could she really be expecting a baby?

Voices grew louder in the hallway, so Serena hurried into the stall. If she took the test, then she could stick it in the bag and look at it later without having to be in here. She had gathered her things earlier, and her duffel bag sat ready by the main door should someone knock and need her to step out.

When she was through, she leaned against the counter, tearing open the lightly sealed envelope, and pulled out the card.

Serena,

Thought you'd like to know before signing the contract. The clerk at the front desk told me that you had been sick. Be sure to drink what I bought for you. It may be the key to save you from needing to run off stage. Even if you feel okay right now, drink it anyway. The taste will be better right now while it's chilled. Please let me know if the answer is positive. I'll be in the dressing room.

Thank you for being a good testimony to my mom. I'm a Christian and have tried to witness to her, but she tunes me out because I'm just her daughter. You really had an affect on her. I saw her reading the paper you gave to her. You're a refreshing light in a sin-darkened world.

Gratefully,
Candace

Serena sighed deeply. The relief of knowing that she was making a difference in someone's life was encouraging. People at church may not see the results of her efforts, but God knew. She thought of Mary, Jesus' mother, and how she pondered things in her heart. "Thank You, God," she whispered. She looked at the front of the stationery once more. A piano stood suspended in the midst of billowy clouds. A bouquet of flowers, tied with lots of ribbon, rested on the bench before it. Serena wondered how Candace ever found such a perfect card. If only she knew how much she enjoyed watching clouds when she had the time.

She slid the card back into its envelope and retrieved the test box from the bag. Someone knocked on the door, and she dropped it back in. "Coming!" she called.

"It's just me, Candy!" She stuck her face in the moment Serena opened the door. "You are first on the schedule tonight!" Candace said with animation. She thrust a bulletin at her. "I hate being so last minute. The stage manager shouldn't have to wait on the office staff. Are you all right?" Candace managed to pause for a moment.

"The card and your inscription meant more than you know...and that you'd take the time to go buy the test for me. I haven't looked at the result yet."

Candace's dark eyes glanced meaningfully at her before she said with energy, "Even if the test isn't positive, you need to guzzle that drink in a hurry. Meet me out here. Only fifteen minutes to go!" Then she was gone.

Serena grabbed the drink and drank it over the sink, so she wouldn't spill any on her dress. She was brushing her teeth again when Candace began pounding on her door. "The MC needs to verify the name of your piece with you, and the makeup artist needs to check you. Come; come! Hurry!" She let herself into the room and seized Serena's overnight bag. "I have it. Just grab the pharmacy bag and follow me."

Serena picked it up, threw her toothbrush into the cosmetic case and zipped it as she raced after her. Candace stuffed Serena's bag into a locker and introduced her to the master of ceremonies. "Serena," she said breathlessly, "this is Mr. Koenig."

Chapter Fifteen

Good and Bad Surprises

Serena felt dazed, as she stood close behind the first curtain while Mr. Koenig walked onto the apron of the stage. The murmur of voices subsided as he greeted the audience. "Good evening! Welcome to the Conservatory's Grand Pianoforte Contest. This is our ninth year hosting this event, and we value your support. With no further ado, permit me to introduce to you Mrs. Serena Callahan. Let's give her a warm reception."

Serena stepped out and walked as gracefully as she could toward the piano. She eased onto the bench, a pleasant smile lighting her face, while Mr. Koenig introduced her composition. "What makes the competition special is that all of the contestants play their own music. The piece Serena will be playing for you tonight is 'Harmonious Praise to God in the key of A.' Enjoy, Folks!"

Serena sat still for a second while she watched him go off stage. Her teacher had taught her to never rush into a performance until she was completely focused. She had said to look at something insignificant to relax her brain. A glimmer of light reflecting off one of the shiny keys caught her eye while she prayed silently, *All for you, Lord, please.* Taking an inconspicuous breath, she found her finger positions and started a tempo in allegro. She barely touched the higher keys as her wrists moved her hands quickly. The notes poured forth from the open piano like the tinkling of a music box.

Our little Allegra—her musical name because I love music... She sure had a personality to match the tempo. Now she's in Heaven with You, Lord. Serena's heart sang along with the beauty of the sonata.

Then her fingers followed each other effortlessly down a harmonic major scale ending in sonorous chords that resounded across the empty stage. *With my whole heart, I say 'yes' to You...for all that You've allowed us to go through.*

With flexible style, her fingers persuaded the melody and the echoing harmony to come alive. *May these people see Jesus in me and desire to glorify Your Son, too.* The music ministered to her own spirit as it helped her pray. She couldn't have put it into words for others how she could play and think of other things besides just the timing and notes, but she was grateful to God for such an outlet. Whenever she was deprived of playing the piano, she wouldn't always realize it...until times like now when the emotional release in the beauty of what He had created swept over her entire being. The biggest contest tonight, and in all of life, wasn't winning but rather beating herself. If she'd only compare herself to God rather than people, He'd work in her His divine plan.

Now she slowed the tempo way down and repeated the music box movement. She caressed the keys tenderly before frolicking into a staccato-filled transition. The higher key of B brought about soul-searching, somber chords again. Serena always thought of the verse in Luke during this part...imagining that she was bowing before God's awesome throne. *Ye are they which justify your-selves before men; but God knoweth your hearts: for that which is highly esteemed among men is abomination in the sight of God.* That was the last thing she wanted—to displease Him by vainly striving for fame and recognition. She thought she was involved in this for the money, but she also knew how deceitful her own heart could be.

She concluded her performance with a dynamic chromatic scale and firm high and low resonating octaves. Serena felt peacefully confident as she stood to bow her head thankfully for the applause. The spotlight beat down unmercifully, and she felt trickles of sweat running down her neck beneath her hair, but her hands felt icy. Mr. Koenig approached her and held his hand out toward her then continued clapping. Serena nodded her head low one more time before walking behind the MC to the safety of the curtains. Mr. Koenig said, "I must save any comments of my own for after all the performances. Now, it is my honor to present to you, Mr. Jonathan Baldwin."

Serena couldn't hear the rest as she entered the dressing room. She yawned as her body craved more oxygen after her diminished breathing while on stage. The makeup lady was busy touching up men and women alike, so their faces wouldn't look like death under the white washing lights. Candace wasn't around, and no one seemed to pay her much mind. She took advantage of the situation to slip back into the lavatory with the pharmacy bag. After locking the door, she nervously pulled out the box.

She suddenly realized that she wanted this to be positive more than anything else. What she had just done was nothing compared to the privilege of being chosen by the God of the universe to bear another life? An impressionable, innocent young mind to be nurtured and cared for was no small task. She slowly pulled out the small wand. "Please, Lord, let it have two lines!"

It did! Serena stared at the pink and white plastic stick. It really did. "Thank You! THANK YOU, GOD!" she cried out. She dropped the box into the trashcan and covered it with paper towels for privacy sake. Hiding the capped test under her arm, she returned to the other room. Serena caught sight of Candace's stylish outfit with a dressy, wintry scarf tied loosely and pinned beneath her left shoulder. She was sitting alone at a desk. Her fingers were intertwined around an insulated, disposable cup--steam rising from its black plastic lid.

Serena sat down beside her. Discreetly, she withdrew the wand and held it against her lap. Candace leaned close to look, her musky perfume lingering in the air. Then she gave her a hug.

"Congratulations, Serena! How I wish that I were in your shoes. My husband and I agreed when we married that we'd delay having children until we were well off and had time to enjoy life. Time has sped by, and we've been married for fifteen years. Lately, I've been noticing cheerful women that are surrounded by loving husbands and busy children and wish we could finally try. Steve, unfortunately, has put having a family out of his mind. We waited too long and have grown accustomed to leading selfish lives. I say 'we' because it was I as well. We like traveling, eating at restaurants and all the rest. How wonderful for you, Serena!"

Serena asked slowly, with apprehension in her voice, "This does mean that I am free from any contracts even if I place, right?"

After Serena came off stage from receiving the second place bouquet, she trudged toward the dormitory alone, the heavy duffel bag banging against her side. The commotion and hum of the crowd was too far away to be heard now, and she felt small in the cold building. She had excused herself from the refreshment festivities so that she could use the bathroom and lock herself into the bedroom before the others came up. What would she have said in response to people's questions anyway now that she'd be disqualified from the tour? By default, the runner up would take her place.

She hoped she could get something nutritious out of the vending machine. She was starting to feel queasy again. If only she didn't have to be stuck here now until she could make arrangements to return home. The word *home* sent chills down her spine and legs. The thought of spending another night in the place was foreboding. She already felt protective of the new life within her. Could it really be true?

Could she and Carl make it without the extra income? Could they afford another baby? She knew she wasn't trusting the Lord, but it was scary.

"Serena!" a voice called after her.

Then little voices yelled, "Mommy!"

Serena dropped everything as she turned around. Running toward her with broad smiles and contagious laughter were her family, and with them were her parents, Jim, and Stephen Eclant. Momentarily they surrounded her. She was hugged and her hands squeezed while, all at once, they tried to congratulate her and tell her how they had worked out their plan.

Then Carl held up his hand. "Silence!" he said loudly with a grin. When everyone was fairly quiet...Joelle and Brookelle clinging to Serena's hands, he turned the explanation over to Jim. "This is all his doing, so we'll let him talk."

Serena looked from one beloved face to the next. Even Stephen wore a mischievous grin. Jim cleared his throat and began. "Miss Serena, now that I'm saved and Stephen teaches me the Bible each week, I've been growing considerably in the Lord. I've also learned a tremendous amount regarding my spiritual life by attending church regularly.

"Well, I confided in Stephen one night that I wished I could do something to thank you and Carl that would mean a lot to you both. He didn't hesitate for a second. He said, 'I'm sure Carl and his girls would love to see Serena compete...as would I. Why don't you and I pay for their tickets and drive up ourselves?' I'm so glad we did. Your performance was fabulous!"

"Directly from the heart," Stephen added.

"Do you have any more commitments tonight, or are you free to go out for ice cream with us?" Carl asked hopefully.

"I'm free," Serena said gladly. "What a marvelous surprise! I'll just stop in the restroom on our way out, then I'll be ready to go."

While she was in the lavatory, she nestled the positive test among the flowers in her bouquet. When she came out, Carl said, "Since we all journeyed from afar to see you tonight," he teased, "we're wondering if we may walk up with you to leave your things. It would be nice to see where you'll be when you're not traveling."

"I don't mind showing you," Serena agreed covertly.

"This is so much fun!" Mom exclaimed. The twins' eyes were lit up, too, with pleasure over the successful plan.

"Were you girls giggling last night when I was on the phone with Daddy because Mr. Eclant and Mr. Jim were at the apartment?"

They answered in unison, "Yes!"

Serena knew they hadn't been in on such a secret before. They were growing up on her. A remorseful pang wrenched her insides.

Dad was standing beside her, so Serena kissed him on the cheek…feeling lighter than she had in a long time. It wasn't like she hadn't tried to help Carl out, but maybe God had some other way in store for her to earn money at home. She walked up beside Carl and took his hand. "This way, everybody!" Once they had all crowded into the dorm room where she had spent the night, Serena hesitated. Should she tell Carl the news long with everyone else? Not seeing any other way of explaining why she wouldn't leave her belongings or come back after eating, she made the announcement, unable to stop smiling.

"Carl, if you'll look in my bouquet, you'll see why I won't be staying here. I'll be going home with you instead if you can make room for me."

No one broke the startled silence as Carl looked through the flowers with a puzzled expression. When he spotted the unique message, he left it where it was. His handsome eyes met Serena's intense gaze, and she nodded her head. "You're going to have a baby?" he asked incredulously.

"Oh!" Dad and Mom cried out in delight.

The twins clapped their hands over their mouths and bounced softly. Carl put his arm around her shoulders and squeezed her close while Joelle and Brookelle ran to Serena and hugged her waist.

"What about the contract?" Carl asked.

"Well, I found out that I wasn't required to sign it unless I placed, and the conservatory recently added a clause stating that pregnancies are not permitted because of physical appearances and safety on the tours. Candace, the stage manager, explained to me that I have the option of staying on here as a paid teacher; or I may choose to have a letter of recommendation written on my behalf to recruit my own students at home."

"Doesn't the conservatory lose out that way?" Mom wondered.

"No. It will bump the man that placed third up into my position, and the honorable mention below him will take his place. Just spending one night here was enough. I can't imagine staying on for an entire year. I was homesick already yesterday, and that was just the first day. I'm sorry I can't help out the way we had planned financially, Carl."

He looked squarely into her apprehensive eyes. "Do not apologize, Serena. That's the most wonderful news you could have told me!" He surveyed the room once more. "God knew that I wouldn't want to leave you here once I saw it. You need to be safe at home and regularly seeing your own doctor."

Relieved, she bent down before the twins. "I've missed too much of your lives already. I couldn't bear to be apart any longer."

When they left the restaurant later, Jim and Stephen bid everyone farewell. "We've both never seen the Statue of Liberty, so we will spend one night here before heading home tomorrow."

"Thank you, two, so very much," Serena said earnestly.

Carl supported Serena's arm over the icy patches as they walked toward Dad and Mom's mini van. "Now I'm sorry we didn't drive separately. Perhaps you would have enjoyed being alone as a family on the trip home," Mom worried.

"You are part of our family, Mom," Carl assured her. "This way, I can snuggle close to my wife while Dad drives," he said, chuckling. He beamed at Serena.

"True!" Dad agreed jovially.

"I'm thrilled that you both came, Mom!" Serena added. "It would have been a waste, anyway, to pay for the extra gas. As you've always said, Mom, I'm your homebody. I feel more secure with family surrounding me. You've made this evening so festive, and the trip will be better because of you." Then playfully, she concluded, "When Carl gets tired, he beats the steering wheel; and it drives me nuts. The more adults to share the driving, the better."

Carl gleefully squeezed her face. "So that's what you think, ha?" He climbed into the back seat to make sure that the girls had buckled up properly before joining Serena in the middle seat. The girls sang quietly to themselves, and Serena kept looking back at them. She couldn't feast her eyes enough on their adorable faces.

Brookelle said, "I'm glad you're going to have a baby."

"Me, too," Joelle agreed. "Will we have a brother or sister?"

All the adults laughed until Serena managed to answer. "I don't know yet. Won't it be fun to be surprised?"

Brookelle spoke again. "Since we are twins, maybe God will give you twins again."

"Yeah," Joelle exhaled. "If they're fraternal rather than identical like we are, we could take turns playing with our brother *and* sister."

"You never know," Carl said. He seemed happier than Serena had ever remembered him. She leaned her head on his shoulder and hoped their family could always stay together just like this.

Serena gladly took up residence again as the queen of their small apartment above a detached house garage in downtown Corning. For a city, it was beautiful. Nestled in among wooded hills, the streets themselves were abundant with mature trees. Carl had been selective about the place they chose. He didn't want to live beside the landlord for privacy's sake, and he didn't want neighbors on the other side of their walls.

The garage was set back from the house that a chiropractor used for his office. No one was there all night, and they were even allowed to park their own car in the garage. There was a separate driveway behind the house for them to use when the doctor and his employees were using the main driveway.

They were twenty minutes from Serena's parents, five minutes from church, and twenty-five minutes from work. Carl had mapped out a route to ride his bike to work in good weather to save on gas, but the apartment was a rare find. He wanted his family to finally have their own haven again...a place where they didn't have to answer to anyone but him. "I'll prove myself to be the loving, spiritual leader and provider my family needs," he had said. He felt more secure at work knowing that his family was safe at home where they belonged. The girls weren't at school where they'd be in danger of guns and knives. He'd rather work several jobs than have Serena gone.

She and the girls kept their rusty station wagon as clean as they could inside despite the winter's snow and mud, and Carl saved on gas by picking up groceries for her each week on his way home from work.

Once the morning sickness--rather "all day sickness"--settled in, Serena snuggled the girls beside her on the futon and schooled them thoroughly. They'd take turns reading aloud from the history, science, and health textbooks and the readers. Each morning she'd dress before waking them. Then while she pulled up the covers on their queen-sized, velour-covered air mattress and straightened up the master bedroom and applied her makeup, the girls would be racing her to get their morning chores finished. Together they'd eat a nutritious breakfast in the kitchen, dining and living combination room.

Serena had arranged the table close to the futon, so the girls sat there to do their workbooks. As they completed each day's assignments, Serena graded them with a red pen and carefully discussed their errors with them individually. If they didn't understand completely, she'd make up extra worksheets or walk to the library with them, after school hours, to find fun books to supplement their learning. She was thrilled to discover the totes that the library compiled, filled with learning games and puzzles as well as books on particular subjects like telling time, counting by fives and tens, and studying leaves.

Serena also joined the local home school support group and took Carl to work on Fridays, so she could have the car. Serena taught piano lessons while Joelle and Brookelle were in gym class. Their instructor was one of the parents who had a phys. ed. degree. The parents took turns setting up field trips, and the one the girls enjoyed most was touring a candy factory. Then Serena had the idea of setting one up through the manufacturing plant where Carl worked. She didn't tell him about it but specifically asked the secretary if she could arrange for the tour to take them past

Carl's machine without telling him ahead of time what group it would be.

Serena woke the girls the morning of the field trip. "Girls, we have to take Daddy to work. It's Friday."

"Group lessons!" the girls exclaimed, rolling off their twin-sized air mattresses.

Serena didn't explain that they were attending a field trip instead of having classes with the other home schoolers at the church. They might accidentally tell. She had already showered and dressed, but the girls knew their routine and headed for the steps. They grabbed their coats off the wall hooks and stepped into their boots on the waterproof mats. They always changed after they got back home.

Carl came in downstairs, stomping his boots, and called up, "Are you about ready? We should probably leave a few minutes early. The streets are snowier than I expected."

"Coming!" the girls yelled, tramping down the wooden steps. Serena followed close behind them with her cosmetic case in hand. She hated to ever waste a moment of time. While Carl drove, she put on her makeup. Then when they got home, she rushed in to get laundry going. She still rejoiced every time she was able to use the washer and dryer without going to the laundromat. Dad had found the set in a used appliance store. He had purchased them for their family's Christmas gift.

Sometimes she still felt as if Miss Emili were looking over her shoulder, wondering why she had done something a certain way. Carl patiently reminded her that she only had to answer to him. He would answer to God for the way he led their family. Miss Emili was out of the picture; but to Serena, she was still very much a part of her thinking process. It was going to take time to heal from the harsh words.

Joelle set the table while Brookelle toasted bread. Serena stood at the countertop buttering it and cooking oatmeal on the hot plate. "I'll give us all our vitamins," Joelle offered, running to the cupboard. Serena watched to be sure she did it correctly. "Thank you," she said, taking the peach-colored prenatal vitamin from her small hand. She bent down to give her a kiss. The girls chewed the flavored animal shapes up while Serena poured the orange juice. After eating and helping the girls dress and do their hair, they headed back toward Carl's workplace.

Serena watched carefully for Carl's expression as the group of twenty students and parents followed the shop foreman toward his noisy machine. He was busy spraying coolant off a large part with an air hose. "Daddy!" the twins called out, but Carl couldn't hear them.

The foreman began talking loudly to be heard. "This machine is the largest in the company. The parts are so heavy that Mr. Callahan here must use the small crane that you see. These metal parts are used for emergency brakes in mining operations and are shipped worldwide. There are many other orders that Mr. Callahan fills such as valve bodies and parts whose applications would be too numerous to list."

Carl turned the hose off and turned around. "I'm sorry, Supervisor. Were you talking to me?" Then he noticed the group and Serena. His expression was classic. He tried to hide his surprise, but Serena knew him too well. He looked back at the job at hand and hooked the crane to the part. Not wanting to seem rude, though, he awkwardly turned back. "Hi, everybody!" he managed politely.

The foreman rewarded him verbally. "This particular employee, Mr. Callahan, is one of our best workers. He's careful and meticulous yet efficient. He doesn't waste any time. Employees like him are helpful to the company and provide themselves better job security by saving us money that we frequently lose because of other workers' careless mistakes."

Serena beamed at Carl. She hoped he saw her in his peripheral vision. One of the dads in the group raised his hand. "Yes, sir?" the supervisor acknowledged.

"What subjects should the children work hard at to be prepared for such a job?"

"Good question. Math. Fractions and decimals...since the parts must be within certain, specific tolerances to fit the machinery they'll be hooked into. Mr. Callahan is dealing with numbers as small as five ten thousanths of an inch. If he doesn't set up and monitor the machining processes precisely, then the expensive parts may need to be scrapped. Thus all the hours we would have paid him for would have been for nothing, as well as the cost of the stock pieces of steel."

"Wow," several of the moms said in unison.

"Another thing a person should have is a good work ethic."

"What's that?" one of the boys called out.

"Work ethic is having developed the behavior of working systematically or in an organized manner. If you are going to succeed in life, you must have moral conduct. That is doing the right thing even when you aren't being watched. I'm Mr. Callahan's foreman, but I don't have to stand over him all day supervising his work. Sometimes he asks me questions or needs me to call a repairman to troubleshoot the machine if it's acting up. Well, let's move on."

Serena felt satisfaction rise in her heart as they walked on. She held back from the rest and smiled at Carl, hoping the gratefulness that she felt being married to him was evident. He looked at her with a questioning smile.

"Yes," Serena informed him. "I set up this field trip. Half an hour more to go, and the buzzer will sound. The girls and I will be waiting in the parking lot for you." She looked around to be sure none of his coworkers were watching before blowing a kiss.

At home, Serena hurried up the steps with Carl chasing her. She collapsed onto the futon, laughing. Carl knelt down on the floor beside her and began tickling her. "I can hardly believe that my wife set me up for 'report card time' in front of twenty people," he growled playfully. The twins piled on top of Serena trying to get in on the fun.

"Whoa!" Carl warned, whisking them both off her legs before they could climb onto her stomach. Then he romped on the floor with them while Serena watched. She felt as if she would burst from overwhelming joy. Reluctantly, she got up to cook supper while Carl sat in his chair to open the mail. "Girls!" she called. "Since we left quite early today, I need you to finish your chores now…like emptying the garbage cans and scouring out the bathroom sink and toilet. Then you may help me with supper."

"Yes, Mommy!" they answered, quickly hopping up from the floor. Serena drew a sudden breath. It still thrilled her whenever she heard that endearing term. She wondered how Blaire and Claire were doing and if they liked the new nanny.

"Honey, please come here," Carl said in a different tone of voice.

Serena shut the cupboard door and set the boxes of macaroni and cheese on the table. "What is it?" she asked as she hurried to sit beside him.

"This letter…" was all he could say as he weakly dropped it into her lap.

She picked it up apprehensively. What more could possibly happen to them? Thoughts whirled as she tried to decipher the unfamiliar handwriting. Carl hadn't filed bankruptcy for testimony's sake. It sure would have made life easier, but they had agreed to sacrifice and simplify in order to keep putting money in the bank for a house. They were still sleeping on air mattresses and cooking with the microwave and hot plate. What would this piece of paper mean to them?

She swallowed hard and stared at the ink until the words came into focus.

March 19, 1999

Carl,

This is to inform you that I am moving out of state to set up a new practice. I need you to be out after thirty days since I have a buyer for the office who needs property tenancy shortly. I apologize for any inconvenience this may cause. You and your family have been excellent to work with. I wish you the best in your venture to find another home.

Kind regards,
Doctor Noyes

Carl sighed. "Rent around here is higher than owning, but there's no way we want to rush into buying a house even though we have enough money for a decent down payment. We could probably find a realtor that would work with a lender on our behalf, but even that's risky since we'll probably have a bad record now after I goofed up and didn't mail that last insurance payment before the house burned. The good thing is, our income to credit ratio is safely into the black. I'm so glad we had decided to apply the forced place coverage insurance claim check toward the house's balance and sell the property.

"You were such a support, Serena, agreeing to put the minimal proceeds we made onto the well and septic bills there. I know it hasn't always been easy for you making ends meet with few belongings. At least the outstanding debts are nearly paid off. Little by little we'll be able to purchase things for our home again."

"Maybe my parents would let us live with them until we can find the right home. Then we wouldn't have to sign a six month contract on a rental property," Serena suggested.

"Absolutely not," Carl said adamantly. His firmness allowed for no arguments. "I'm not going that route to put you under the stress of having two authorities."

The girls paused at the kitchen trashcan with the bedroom wastebaskets in their hands. Serena knew they sensed their concern. She tried to smile reassuringly.

Then Carl had an impromptu suggestion. "Why don't we all go for a hike on one of the State Forest trails? The fresh air and exercise will do us all good."

The girls shouted their approval and raced to return the wastebaskets to their places. "We'll all feel hungrier when we get home, too," Serena agreed. Carl went downstairs first to get the car warming up. The girls had put their coats on, and Serena had just slid into hers when the phone began to ring.

She followed the girls down the steps. She didn't feel like talking to whoever it was. She wanted to enjoy her own family right now. If she happened to slip and briefly mention the decision they were agonizing over, the person would most likely reply with a bigger and better story. She just couldn't bear that...not right now. She'd been bearing those stories for years it seemed. Whenever they had another wave of trials hit them, other people seemed to think their tiny waves were larger and interrupted to tell about them.

Serena always wondered why people couldn't simply say, "I empathize with you. I'll be praying..." instead of hogging the conversation for ten minutes, expounding upon every detail of their burdens. It had happened so numerously that Serena found herself forgetting the manners she had been reared with and defensively treating people the same way.

Mom and Jerusha were the only two she knew who had learned the grace of being good listeners--besides Carl. The phone continued to ring as a wave of bitterness toward Bethany swept over her. She had tried to be there for her when she needed to vent about her marital problems.

She had bitten her tongue several times.

Finally she had been convicted that she wasn't helping Bethany but was actually encouraging unbiblical attitudes toward her husband by attending to her. She informed Bethany that Mr. Jasmine also had a side from which to argue. Bethany exhibited controlled anger at the unexpected news and said fervently, "Haven't I stayed with him for all these years?"

"Yes," Serena agreed, "but you haven't endeavored to put your heart into it with the goal that your marriage will work. You've only been enduring, and your husband knows that. It's just time for me to be honest. Isn't that what true friends are for?"

Bethany said cruelly, "You don't understand because you've never had to go through anything like this." Then she walked away as if out of her life and could care less.

That day had been like a nightmare. How could Bethany understand that she *had* experienced heartaches that were so deep she could hardly breathe? Precious Allegra would never be in their home again. They were struggling to pay for things that were bygones, and Serena was under Miss Emili's strict perfectionism then as well. Not to mention the withdrawal from her twins she had experienced day after day.

Bethany's husband had paid off all her expensive medical loans and had provided her with a mansion home. Bethany loved hostessing and volunteering in the community. Her name and prestige meant more to her than anything else. Serena worried, though, that she was becoming the same as Bethany by not being willing to learn from others. She was becoming bitter toward anyone who wouldn't understand. She knew she needed to be cleansed from the awful root of bitterness before it ruined herself.

"Please help me, God, to know how to sort out these emotions and rest in You completely," she begged. "I want to be like Jesus...how He could genuinely call Judas Iscariot 'Friend' as he was betraying Him. I can't comprehend that kind of forgiveness."

The trails were shady, so there was plenty of snow rather than mud. They saw several cross country ski tracks, but they didn't stay out long since the days were still short, and the air was chilly...feeling colder as time went by.

Serena picked up the boxes of macaroni and cheese off the table and noticed the answering machine flashing. She pressed the playback button. "Serena, this is Suzanne Patton. I have an important matter to discuss with you if you'll kindly return my call." Serena grabbed a sticky paper and one of the girls' pencils. She scribbled down the number then replayed the message to verify it.

After she got the water heating on the hot plate, she asked Carl to keep an eye on it. Then she took the cordless handset to the bedroom where it would be quiet. "Hello, Serena!" the young woman exclaimed. "I'm so relieved that you called me back so promptly. Once something's on my mind, I can't get it out until it's taken care of. Remember the young man I told you about that was interested in me?" She paused for a response.

"I do," Serena answered.

"Well, I've tried to be open-minded about him--doing my best not to lead him on until I was sure. I've pictured myself as his encourager, and if I could...or really want to be…a crown to HIM for the rest of my life. Thank you for your prayers. God allowed some circumstances to happen in front of me that proved his character is weak. He quit a good job because he thought something my dad said to another man at church alluded to his dislike of the company.

"Then when a group of us from church passed out flyers and decided to go out to eat afterwards, he wasn't prepared. Instead of gracefully bowing out and leaving, he came along and let another girl pay for his food.   I personally need a man who can think for himself and plan ahead."

"I completely agree, Suzanne. You've got wisdom. It sounds like a lack of training on the parents' part."

"That's what I've been noticing, too. His mother seems to baby him and is always praising him to anyone who will listen. God has brought someone very special into my life that is all I've ever longed for. The more I'm around him, the more I forget I ever liked Dominic...if that makes any sense."

"It makes perfect sense, Suzanne. A woman should never rush into marriage just for the novelty of being a wife. There's a lot more to it than that." Serena searched her memory for a clue as to who the young man could be.

Suzanne didn't keep her wondering. "Jim, your neighbor down here, has been growing so much. He and Stephen spend a lot of time together; and my dad counsels him, too. Jim has become like a member of the family to us, and Dad really believes he has a sincere heart. I had to call you since you cared so much. Now you'll know more specifically how to pray for me. Is all well with you?"

"Thank you for asking, Suzanne. The apartment we are renting is going to be sold shortly, so we are looking for another place to live."

"Is it okay with you if I mention this at prayer meeting this week?"

"That'd be great! Keep me posted, Suzanne, on you and Jim. How exciting! It was nice of you to call." Serena hung up feeling blessed to have such a sweet friend.

Carl fasted and prayed the following day at work, and Serena and the girls took turns praying before they ate breakfast and lunch. Could this really be happening? Serena felt drained. She forced herself to be joyful around the girls. Their family was growing, yet they were virtually home-less. She had underlined many verses in her Bible that seemed to stand out regarding her circumstances. Little by little, she was working on memorizing them.

Verses in Joshua chapter twenty-four kept running through her mind the most. "Ye dwelt in the wilderness a long season. Now therefore fear the LORD, and serve him in sincerity and in truth. For the LORD our God, he it is that brought us up... from the house of bondage...and preserved us in all the way wherein we went."

For the next several days after receiving Doctor Noyes's letter, they looked at ads in the paper and drove around Corning and surrounding areas, stopping at realtors' offices for leads on suitable rental properties. It seemed impossible to find another situation like the place they were in. Discouraged, Carl and Serena discussed their options in regards to the few apartments that even looked halfway workable. "Doctor Noyes was giving us a good deal, I'm finding out." Carl sighed.

When Serena climbed onto the air mattress later that night, Carl was already asleep. The baby was beginning to take up more space, so she had to lie on her side. Carl hadn't exhibited any optimism that evening which made her feel weak with dismay, inhibiting her ability to swallow much food. She had forced some down with milk for the baby's sake, but she still felt hopeless. She quietly leafed through her Bible she had laid under the nightlight that was plugged into the wall.

It was the seventh day of the month, so she began reading in Psalm chapter seven, then chapter seventeen. Before long, she reached Psalm one hundred seven. The words, starting in verse four, began to jump out at her. *They wandered in the wilderness in a solitary way; they found no city to dwell in. ...their soul fainted in them. Then they cried unto the LORD in their trouble, and he delivered them out of their distresses. And he led them forth by the right way, that they might go to a city of habitation. Oh that men would praise the LORD for his goodness, and for his wonderful works to the children of men!*

She began to cheer up the farther she read. *He sent his word, and healed them, and delivered them from their destructions. They...are at their wits' end. Then are they glad because they be quiet; so he bringeth them unto their desired haven. (He) setteth the poor on high from affliction, and maketh him families like a flock.*

Serena prayed that she and Carl would be at rest in Christ even if their desired haven wouldn't be a reality until Heaven. She fell asleep then with peace in her heart.

Carl came home with egg boxes the next afternoon. Serena had the girls bring them from the living room into the kitchen, and she reluctantly packed all the dishes she could spare. The paper plates Carl had bought would suffice temporarily. She tried to console herself that at least she didn't have years of accumulation to pack like many people. They were living so sparsely as it was. Carl asked, "Are you all right?"

"Why do you ask?"

"You're quieter than usual."

She said, "I can't help wondering if I should have stayed on at the conservatory and taught lessons. Then maybe we'd be..." she hesitated, feeling confused.

"Be what, Serena? Nothing would be better with you gone, and you've told me several times not to look back when I get down. Isn't that right?"

Wishing she didn't have to answer, she softly said, "Yes."

Carl continued with fervency, "If it makes you feel any better, I believe God orchestrated all the events for me to be there and for you to realize that you were expecting this baby for your own safety." He laid his hand on her extended stomach and began to pray, "Dear God, help us to live the way we believe...that You are sovereign. We commit our lives to You and ask that You'll give us the strength to be content and accepting of whatever You provide for our lives. Lord, we're claiming the promise in Your Word that righteousness delivers even when riches are unprofitable.

"Please reassure Serena that her obedience to You by being a keeper at home is better than sacrifice. Saul was anointed king over Israel when he was little in his own sight; but later...when he feared the people and sinfully obeyed their voice rather than Yours, the kingdom was rent from him. May we be humble and regard this seemingly impossible task as a compliment from You, God. Since You're counting us worthy of this situation, we're trusting You for an answer as to where we should move."

Serena clung to him as he prepared to follow up on some part-time job leads. "Carl...you spoke a word in due season. Thank you. I feel much better. Please drive safely," she pleaded. "All four of us need you." She caressed her belly protectively as she watched him back out of the driveway from the upstairs window. Joelle and Brookelle were on either side, respectfully quiet, sensing her frame of mind.

"Well, Girls, let's hustle and see how much we can accomplish."

They saved one large saucepan, one frying pan and eight complete settings of silverware. Joelle wrapped the few knick-knacks carefully in clean dishtowels, and the kitchen was done. They made quick work of the girls' room. Serena knelt down and selected several outfits that could be rematched with each other to change their appearances. Everything else, they carefully removed from the hangers and laid as neatly as possible lengthwise in a box. Brookelle wrote on the boxes with a permanent marker as Serena spelled the words to her that she couldn't sound out.

The downstairs door thumped shut as they were settling the last of the medicinal supplies into a box of bath towels. All three of them rushed to greet Carl at the top of the stairs. A grin illuminated his face, and he looked younger than he had before he left.

"What is it?" Serena wondered.

"We won't have to leave Corning...*yet* anyway. I have the job as dishwasher at the Luxury Hotel. They were also in need of a housekeeper on the third floor. Lucinda's Restaurant in Ohio gave me such a good recommendation that they listened when I asked if you could have that job as well. Instead of dismissing my unusual request, the manager agreed to give us a four-person room in exchange for both of our pay. I didn't think you'd object, so they already gave me the key. Our room number is 96. How about that? The year we were married?"

Serena was apprehensive. "But what about the girls? Will it be a problem for them to be with me?"

Carl's smile grew. "I verified everything I thought you'd possibly ask. The management is fine with our situation as long as the girls are unobtrusive. I assured Chris that our girls are little ladies." He bent down to hug them.

"Yes, Daddy!" Brookelle sang out. "We'll be good helpers."

Joelle enthused, "We get to live in a hotel! It'll be so much fun just like when we went to Lancaster with Grandpa and Grandma and bought our baby doll quilts!"

Chapter Sixteen

New Church Family

That weekend, they moved most of their boxes into the garage at Serena's parents'. Mom was frustrated that they wouldn't stay at their house. Carl reassured her that they'd be better off than in the apartment. "We won't be paying other than by our perspiration and some elbow grease, so we'll be putting more money into the bank for the future. We like the Corning area, and you are still helping us out tremendously by granting us free storage until we can move into something larger and more permanent."

Serena supported Carl and was thankful to have a place to live, but she prayed that they'd be able to have their own place before the baby came.

It wouldn't be easy living so close to others and keeping such a full schedule...especially once she were nursing the little one. Serena settled the room's dressers and made it feel as much like home as possible Sunday afternoon in between church services. She put a tablecloth over the small table and arranged the hot plate and cooking supplies on the counter against the wall. She scoured out the tub, toilet and sink thoroughly with her own disinfectant cleaners before she unpacked their toothbrushes and other toiletries.

Carl helped her fold up most of the hotel bedding from both mattresses. Then he shook open clean new lawn bags and held them one by one as Serena slid the flat sheets, bedspreads, then and the pillows inside. Carl twisted and tied them shut, and the girls stowed them neatly in the far corner of the room beyond their bed against the wall. Serena made up the beds again, over the existing fitted sheets that she had left on, with their own sheets, comforters and pillows. Carl carried up their small microwave from the car, and Serena heated some cans of ready-to-serve soup in a plastic pan before freshening up for the evening church service.

They arrived fifteen minutes early. Pastor Reynolds greeted them as he made his rounds. "Good evening, Folks. Did your move go all right?"

"Yes, Pastor. Thank you," Carl responded. "We appreciated your offer to help us, but it went quite smoothly." He flashed a heartfelt smile.

Pastor Reynolds seemed relieved. "I'm glad to hear that. We're praying earnestly for you at home and every Tuesday morning in our men's meeting."

"That means so much," Serena added.

The elderly preacher looked directly at her. "I hate to ask this of you when you've had such a busy weekend," he began in his meek way, "but Mrs. Mapes came down with the flu this afternoon. You've played the piano beautifully in the past for your family's special music, so she mentioned to me that perhaps you'd be comfortable with playing the congregationals. If it's too difficult being put on the spot like this, then please, by all means, say 'no.'"

"I'd be glad to, Pastor." Serena squeezed Carl's hand before hurrying up front to look over the song director's list. She figured out an offertory and began the prelude.

As Serena made her way back to the pew after the singing, she thought about how gentle and sincere Pastor Reynolds was. She wondered if his personality would have been similar to Moses' in the Old Testament. Pastor preached solid messages from the Bible while making the people feel that he cherished them like a loving dad would. He wasn't a flatterer or a men pleaser, but he was openly joyful at the people's presence.

When Serena joined Carl again, he pointed to the text in his Bible. "II Timothy Chapter Three." Pastor Reynolds was reading verse five. "'Having a form of godliness, but denying the power thereof: from such turn away.' Folks, in the last days, the Bible says in verse thirteen that evil men and seducers shall wax worse and worse, deceiving, and being deceived. Look in chapter four, verses three and four. 'For the time will come when they will not endure sound doctrine; but after their own lusts shall they heap to themselves teachers, having itching ears; 'And they shall turn away their ears from the truth, and shall be turned unto fables.'

"We need to be diligent and love Christ's appearing. It's closer than it's ever been before. Don't let down your guard, dear people. We can't allow ourselves to be turned from the Scriptures. The scary thing is, seemingly 'spiritual' people may be those who try the hardest to pull you down. If you don't think so, remember the chief priests and scribes who stood and vehemently accused Jesus. Don't you think it was pride that made the elders of the people despise Him even after all the healing He had done? The captains of the temple were glad to covenant money to Judas Iscariot.

"Before we judge them too harshly, let's search our own hearts. If someone better than we came into our midst today, would we welcome that person with open arms? Or would we look for an opportunity to criticize him or her so we wouldn't lose face? Jesus Himself washed the disciples' feet and said, 'He that is greatest among you, let him be as the younger; and he that is chief, as he that doth serve.' Often times opinionated, outgoing people tend to leave no room for the opinions of quieter personalities.

"Psalm 101:5 says, 'Whoso privily slandereth his neighbour, him will I cut off: him that hath an high look and a proud heart will not I suffer.' I'm sure every one of us is guilty. I Samuel 2:3—'Talk no more so exceeding proudly; let not arrogancy come out of your mouth: for the LORD is a God of knowledge, and by him actions are weighed.' Of course, our labor isn't in vain in the Lord. We only amount to anything because of His purpose and grace. Some of us may only be wooden or earthen vessels rather than golden or silver, but may we be found honorable.

"Do we express deep, edifying love and concern for others' difficulties and needs, or are we impatient and filled with strife? Our words are so important because someday we may need to eat them. Please look with me at John 5:44 where

Jesus was speaking in the temple. It reads, 'How can ye believe, which receive honour one of another, and seek not the honour that cometh from God only?' Jesus spoke of Himself in verse forty-one, 'I receive not honour from men.'

"First Corinthians 7:23-24 says, 'Ye are bought with a price; be not ye the servants of men. 'Brethren, let every man, wherein he is called, therein abide with God.' In Psalm 103, 'Bless the LORD...ye ministers of his, that do his pleasure.' Am I, are you, remembering His commandments? The Bible promises the Lord's pity and mercy to those who fear him. Fear isn't always a bad thing, Folks. A healthy respect and reverence is necessary."

Serena sat in awe at the way God had blessed this man with amazing preaching ability. She soaked up every verse and underlined them in her Bible to look at again later.

"In closing," he continued, "Job said to his friends, 'Behold, the fear of the Lord, that is wisdom; and to depart from evil is understanding.' His friends had been foolish and did not speak right things like Job. God's wrath was kindled against the three. Elihu had said to Job, 'Take heed, regard not iniquity: for this hast thou chosen rather than affliction.' He was wrong, though. He didn't know Job's heart. Not everyone that's suffering is in the hard place because they're sinning and not willing to endure hardness.

Job said, 'I am righteous...Should I lie against my right? Miserable comforters are ye all. Shall vain words have an end? Or what emboldeneth thee that thou answerest? I could also speak as ye do: if your soul were in my soul's stead, I could heap up words against you, and shake mine head at you. Thou hast made desolate all my company. How forcible are right words! but what doth your arguing reprove? Do ye imagine to reprove words...of one that is desperate, which are as wind? Cannot my taste discern perverse things? I know that thou wilt not hold me innocent. No doubt but ye are the people, and wisdom shall die with you.'

"Isn't that interesting?" Pastor Reynolds interjected. "Some people and administrations seem to think they've arrived. What on Earth did previous generations do without them? Anyway, Job went on, '...I have understanding as well as you.' Isn't that true? Any Christian who's sincerely seeking after the Lord and studying His Word can grow. Then Job said, 'I am not inferior to you...I am as one mocked of his neighbour, who calleth upon God, and he answereth him.' How would we like it if someone answered us in God's stead?

"'O that ye would altogether hold your peace! and it should be your wisdom. He will surely reprove you, if ye do secretly accept persons. Though he slay me, yet will I trust in him: but I will maintain mine own ways before him. He also shall be my salvation: for an hypocrite shall not come before him.' You see, Job's friends were wiser when they didn't speak but wept in mourning and simply sat with him to comfort him.

Don't get me wrong. We don't have any excuse to sin, though. Anything we do is because of God's strength, so may He 'make you to increase and abound in love one toward another...'To the end he may stablish your hearts unblameable in holiness before...our Father, at the coming of our Lord Jesus Christ with all his saints.' Try to memorize John 13:35 this week."

He called on one of the men to close in prayer while Serena hurried to the piano to play the invitational song. Then she followed the other parishioners down the aisle toward Carl where he stood off to the side waiting for her.

The next Sunday morning, the twins met them in the foyer as Carl held Serena's coat for her. They stood close together to stay out of the way while others made their way toward the outside door. Serena buttoned up while Carl pulled theirs off the hangers. "How was Sunday School?" he asked while he held the purple coats out.

"Good," Joelle said. "We learned about Ruth."

"Yes," added Brookelle. "Ruth had lost her husband and was in a valley...but not to stay. Mrs. Barletta said that because all the city, including Boaz, knew she was virtuous, she wasn't under *repoach*. Is that how you say it?" she queried.

Carl grinned lovingly. "*Reproach*," he said, over-emphasizing the *r*.

"Carl, Serena," someone spoke.

All four of them turned their heads. It was sweet Mrs. Barletta. She was beautiful with her feminine outfit and tastefully applied makeup. Her hair framed her face in soft curls, and her gentle personality attracted everyone to her. She held her Two-year-old son in her arms. "Serena, I was wondering how you're feeling...if you are past the sick stage yet?"

Serena nodded and sighed in relief. "Yes. Praise God." Her white teeth illuminated her face.

Mrs. Barletta quickly added, "Joelle and Brookelle were telling me about your new adventure." Her tone was kind yet uncertain. "I hope you don't mind their telling me, but I had hoped to have you over for lunch today. I asked the girls what plans they thought you might have for the afternoon, and they bubbled over with joy to inform me of your recent move. You must be exhausted. If you'd rather go back to your room and get some well-deserved rest, we'll completely understand. My husband and I just thought we'd extend an invitation if you don't feel like cooking." She hastened to assure them, "If not now, we'll be sure to get together soon. It will be good to get to know you better."

Serena glanced at Carl. He only shrugged and said, "It's up to you, Honey."

The teacher politely excused herself, saying, "We'll meet up with you in the parking lot after you've had a chance to decide."

The lunch was delicious turkey stroganoff, sliced cucumbers and brownies with ice cream and fruit. Alice Barletta was a gracious hostess, making them feel at home. She was calm and sat at the table with them as if she had all the time in the world to fellowship. Chuck Barletta carried little Timmy away on his back for his nap, and Alice watched with a smile. Turning back to her guests, she asked, "So you girls will help me with the puppets next week?"

Joelle and Brookelle looked up eagerly from their desserts. "Yes, Mrs. Barletta!" they agreed in unison.

"If that's okay with you," the lady verified. "Whenever I use the puppets for a lesson, I'll call you a few days prior since they'll need to be half an hour early to practice their lines."

"Not a problem," Carl said affably.

"The girls will anticipate it all week," Serena agreed.

Chuck returned and came around the table with the coffee pot. Alice passed the cream and flavored creamers without taking her eyes off her students. "Do you girls remember what we learned this morning?"

Joelle spoke first. "Because Ruth was unselfish and willing to leave family and the comforts of her familiar homeland, Naomi--her mother-in-law, wanted Ruth to be blessed and find rest in Bethlehem."

"Boaz, a mighty kinsman of wealth, was friendly and kind to the stranger. He said to Ruth, 'The LORD recompense thy work, and a full reward be given thee of the LORD God of Israel, under whose wings thou art come to trust.' That's our new memory verse," Brookelle concluded.

Alice shook her head in amazement. "However do your girls retain knowledge so well?"

"It's because they're home educated," Chuck answered convincingly.

"Oh, yes! I'd love for you to tell me all about that," Alice pleaded. "Timmy is the only child we'll be able to have, and we intend to do our best by him."

Serena swallowed her sip of amaretto-flavored coffee. "Timmy is well-behaved, so that's very much in your favor...along with your evident organizational skills. The regulations vary from state to state; but in New York--once a child is six years old, the parents must send an annual letter of intent to the school district before July first. The district will subsequently provide an individualized home instruction plan (IHIP) form that you must return within four weeks or by August 15th. That plan must contain a list of the syllabi, curriculum materials, textbooks or instruction plans for each required subject along with the name of the instructor.

"Then as the school year progresses, the parents are required to submit quarterly reports by the dates they indicated on the IHIP. Those reports will contain a description of the material covered in each subject and either a grade or written evaluation for each."

Carl added, "When you send in your fourth quarterly report, you must simultaneously submit an annual assessment that's based on results of a commercially published norm-referenced achievement test administered by a New York State certified teacher. Alternative forms of assessments may be accepted if they meet regulatory requirements. The superintendent has the authority to approve other arrangements."

"Wow!" Chuck exclaimed. "How could anyone think of home schooling as a fly by night operation? Parents must really be committed to take on such a work load."

"Yes," Serena said. "Unfortunately, there are some who give us all a bad name by sloughing off and ultimately sending their children back to public school after they've lapsed behind. Most parents, however, teach their own children because they care more than anything about them. Doctors, lawyers--down to the poor," she paused to smile in acknowledgement of herself, "are willing to sacrifice time and money...while still paying school taxes...to provide their youngsters a safe, loving atmosphere of scholastic excellence."

Mrs. Barletta nodded. "How can one on one teaching be beat? I'd love to see the textbooks you use sometime if you don't mind."

"Not at all. It'd be my pleasure," Serena assured her. "There are many choices when it comes to curriculum. We purchase all ours from an accredited college in Florida. Their books are phenomenal! The artwork and photos throughout the texts are colorful and interesting, and the subjects are intricately correlated."

Carl carried on the conversation while Serena finished her coffee. "Yes. For instance, the work pages in the spelling book may have sentences that will remind the child about his studies in science. The math word problems may be reminiscent of what is being currently learned in history. We also receive many catalogs in the mail from other companies that provide extra curricular helps and visuals. There's a wealth of information out there."

"Must the parents be certified teachers?"

"No, Alice," Carl answered. "We must only be competent, which we're deemed if we follow the regulations."

"Are there guidelines for the subjects?" Chuck wondered.

Carl said, "All of those are listed in the copy of the regulations the school district sends...the three r's, of course; geography; United States history; health and phys. Ed.; music; and visual arts...along with patriotism; substance abuse; highway safety and traffic regulation; fire prevention and safety; et cetera."

When Serena helped Alice carry the dishes into the kitchen, she asked carefully, "You mentioned that Timmy will be your only little one. Do you care to talk about it? I only ask because I know from losing my daughter that it helps to be able to vent sometimes. Please don't feel pressured though."

Alice eased her armload of glasses down onto the counter and exclaimed, "You sweetheart!

No one at church has ever asked me that before. I've begun to realize that usually only those people who have experienced similar trials know how to relate to others who are grieving."

Serena nodded. "I was wondering what grief you had gone through because you've been so considerate of us since we began attending after our move from Ohio."

"I sensed a common bond as well," Alice stated, turning to open the dishwasher. "Well, my cervix had to be stitched; and I was on bed rest for seven months of the pregnancy. After Timmy was born, my uterus didn't get back to normal. I was in a lot of pain, and an exam revealed that my uterus was nearly falling out. The doctor tried his best, but I ended up having a partial hysterectomy. I'm so thankful that Chuck had taken oodles of pictures of me during every stage of the pregnancy. I savor every newborn picture, and we continue to be 'camera happy.'

"We know several ladies who have never been able to have any children. One of them is now dealing with the hassles of foster care in hopes of adopting a child or siblings. Another friend is enduring the extreme invasion of privacy as they're working through an adoption agency. They are getting their baby girl from China. The baby was born a year ago, but the paperwork is far from done. They've been told it may be eight more months before they may fly over to get her from the orphanage. They've sent several packages of clothing and toys for her. They get pictures of her in return, but I can't imagine losing the entire precious bonding of the first two years. They've been prepared financially and on time with every required document, but still their patience must be tried day in and day out as the time ticks by.

"Someone always has something worse than I do. I try to think of Jesus and the ultimate sacrifice He made for me, but I still can't help mourning the fact that little Timmy will never have brothers or sisters. I don't want him to feel lonely." Alice paused to wash her hands, and tears glistened in her soft brown eyes.

Serena squeezed her shoulder before bending down to load the plates.

Alice dried her hands and said, "I always longed to have a girl, too. How much fun it would be to dress her and fuss with her hair. You know how people say that a daughter is always a daughter, but a son is only a son until he marries? I'll tell you, we're praying earnestly for a daughter-in-law that will consider us like her own family. I always worry, too, that we'll baby Timmy without meaning to. It's hard, you know, when he is our baby for good."

Serena probed carefully. "You won't consider adoption as well?"

"Chuck says that the only way we'll adopt is if a child in need is offered to us privately in a closed adoption. He doesn't want to lose a moment of quality time with our son. Serena, I could just cry when I see how hard Chuck tries to train and play with him. He takes him everywhere he goes if at all possible. He had dreamed of having a large family. He never says a word to make me feel badly, but I can't help thinking that I let him down."

Tears spilled from Serena's eyes as she imagined being in Alice's shoes. She set the last plate in the dishwasher, stood up and said, "So many times, the only way I deal with my grief over losing Allegra is to remember the sovereignty of God. He could have prevented her death. The Bible says that children have guardian angels. Where was hers that evening? I know it's not the same at all as having your own girls, but you are welcome to visit us anytime. Timmy can play with Joelle and Brookelle; and when this new baby arrives, you may hold him or her for as long as you wish."

Alice hugged her and held on. She pressed her moist face against Serena's hair and whispered, "God bless you." Her body shook as she cried quietly.

Serena patted her back and, for the first time, realized that she was thankful for the sorrow she had experienced. Tears hadn't always been quick to come even when she had wanted to cry. Her loss had enabled her to 'weep with those that weep.'

Chapter Seventeen

Hotel Life

On a Thursday, nearly two weeks later, Serena was working down through the last hallway of rooms. Joelle recited her spelling words aloud while Serena scoured a tub. Her tummy had grown large enough now that it was awkward to reach. She wiped at her perspiring forehead with her sleeve, careful not to touch her face with her long rubber gloves. Serena looked down at the book propped up against the wall on a clean section of floor. "Spell *purse*," she said, looking at her first grader with a thrill of joy that pulsed through her body. It was still hard to believe at times that she was really working with her own daughters again. She wondered how Claire and Blaire were making out. Were they with a new nanny or enrolled in kindergarten?

"*Purse*," Joelle repeated. "*P, u, r, s, e. Purse.*"

"Correct," Serena praised, her eyes glowing. "*Round.*" She skimmed several words down the list mentally, so she could ask and listen to them without turning her head every few seconds. With her large cleaning cup, she thoroughly rinsed the porcelain with hot water. Carefully holding onto the edge, she pushed herself into a standing position. She pulled the curtain and proceeded to the mirror and sink.

Joelle needed a little help with the sight word *give*. She omitted the *e*. Serena explained that normally the rule was to pronounce the vowel with a long sound if the word ended with an *e*, but this word was one she had to memorize since it broke that rule. The *i* was short.

Joelle completed the list, and Brookelle had already recited the same words to Serena earlier. Now they both stood against the wall behind her. She could watch them in the mirror as she held a miniature spelling bee. "Spell *loose*." With a soapy finger, Serena wrote a tally mark under *Brooke* on the glass. Joelle easily spelled the next trick word...*lose*. A mark glided beneath *Jo*. When Joelle misspelled *chalk*, Brookelle was baffled.

After a moment of silence, Serena looked up from wiping the faucet handles.

She jumped as she saw a fourth face in the mirror. The manager hastened to apologize. "I'm sorry for startling you. I just wanted to tell you that someone anonymously delivered bags of groceries and things for you to the front desk. I was wondering if you'd like for me to have someone from room service deliver them to your room after you're through cleaning, or if you'd rather have Carl get them on his way up later?"

Serena stared into the mirror until she came to her senses and turned to face the man. "Oh, uh...yes...mmm...well, they might be in the way behind the desk. I know you'd only send someone you trust with them. I'll call down to the desk once I'm finished. Wait a minute...I'll just get them. There's no reason to inconvenience anyone else. Thank you for your thoughtfulness."

"It won't be an inconvenience," Chris convinced her, "though I hadn't thought about someone stealing from the bags. You're right. It wouldn't be good since you don't know what you have yet...should something disappear. I will bring everything up myself."

"Thank you, Chris," Serena said lamely. She felt badly for causing him an extra task, but she knew better than to discourage his display of gentlemanliness. She was glad, too, not to have to wait hours for Carl's return.

Chris called back over his shoulder, "Call my pager when you're ready."

Serena and the girls waited in the hall just outside their door. Chris came around the corner from the elevator promptly. He was lugging two heavy bags slung over his forearms and balancing a weighty box in his hands. Serena swung open the door and held it for him but remained outside the room for appearance's sake. Chris looked back. "Where do you want these?"

"On the table will be fine," Serena answered gratefully. She watched as he slid the box from his hands and lifted the bags one at a time from his weary arms. "They've left marks in my skin," he chuckled as he came back out rubbing them.

Serena said, "I appreciate it, Chris."

"That's not all of it."

"Really?"

"Really. I'll bring a dolly this time though." He smiled.

When he returned, Serena asked him if he'd seen the person who had dropped everything off. He shook his head. "Nope. The receptionist took care of it all. I was on a conference call in my office."

The girls were bright-eyed as they stood on either side of her after they had said good evening to the manager and locked themselves in the room. Serena gazed at the full table and cluttered floor all around it. Then she knelt down and began to pray aloud. She felt the air stir as the twins got down, too. "God, we thank You for the generous person who sacrificed to bring so much. Please bless him or her in a special way, and may we put to wise use all that we've received. We won't forget Your provision."

She got onto her feet and used her knees to straighten back up. "Girls, we'll take turns looking in the bags. Brookelle, since you won the spelling bee, you may go first."

Slowly she eased her hand into the closest one. Grasping something, she pulled out a jumbo package of coated paper plates.

"Oh!" Serena exclaimed approvingly. "How helpful since we don't have a kitchen!"

Brookelle eagerly reached in.faster this time. She retrieved Styrofoam cups. Next came sturdy plastic ware and napkins. The last item was a quality hand can opener. Serena shook her head, trying to shake the feeling that she were in a dream. Taking the empty bag, she felt the plastic as she folded it neatly. It crinkled. This had to be a real life experience. She nodded to Joelle who wondered with her eyes if she could take her turn.

There were boxes of dried soup packets, flavored instant oatmeal and creamy wheat. The girls squealed when they saw their favorite cheesy puffed rice snacks. Fig cookies, molasses and chewy lemon and soft oatmeal cookies in their boxed, wrapped packaging tempted their appetites now that they noticed their growling tummies. Still more, there were boxed whole-wheat crackers and spray cheese, teriyaki beef jerky, vitamins, and disposable bowls.

Serena showed the girls how to fold that bag, and then she dug into a box. They oohed and aahed over each item. Serena began telling the girls where to put things away, so they could keep order. They stacked the cans of meat-filled pasta, fruit, pudding, and stew behind the curtains on the wide windowsills along with the can opener. Serena helped them carry two boxes of bottled spring water over to the coat rack. They shoved them under it, close to the wall.

Joelle was surprised when she opened a large gift bag. "Mommy! Earrings and necklaces and dolls...and clothes!"

Serena plopped down onto her bed and began sobbing. "Lord, I'm completely overwhelmed!" She looked around the stocked room as unworthiness began to hover like a foreboding cloud. "I don't deserve this."

Brookelle pulled out an envelope next and handed it to her.

It was lightly sealed and easy to open. The card was homemade. The large bubble letters were a warm red shade, and spelled, **GOD'S GENTLENESS MAKES US GREAT.** Then in smaller bubble print, rather than handwriting, the givers had typed, **We think of you as angels in our lives as you live the fresh fragrance of the Holy Spirit. We know that takes sticking by the stuff...performing menial jobs day by day.**

Please don't feel badly about our fun shopping spree. We are the blessed ones. We've been on the receiving end before, and please know that this is intended to relieve some pressures so that you may focus on the little joys of parenthood. Don't overlook today for a better future. Try to see the wonder in life as your girls do. God will bless you and keep you!

Loving Christian Friends

Serena didn't brush at the torrent of tears. Her girls wrapped their little arms tightly around her neck. "It's okay, Mommy," Brookelle comforted. Joelle retrieved the box of tissues, whipping some out as she ran back.

When Carl came in later, the girls were sleeping peacefully. As he always did, Carl bent over to kiss each daughter on her forehead. He was never in a rush, but savored the fragrance of their clean hair and their quiet breathing. Sometimes they were awake or just barely asleep and would rouse to hug him and tell him about their day. The girls slept on contentedly, and Carl kissed Serena tenderly before wrapping his arms around Serena's expanding waste. "How's this little one doing?" he asked then pressed his hand there, hoping to be rewarded by a little kick.

Serena beamed at him. "Wonderful! Didn't you notice the girls' new lightweight p.j.'s with the playful kitten print?"

Carl looked back over his shoulder. "No. Where did they get those?"

Serena took him by the hand and led him around the room. "Someone who knows we live here now delivered this variety anonymously to the main desk. Don't you think it'd have to be dear Alice Barletta?"

Carl raised his eyebrows uncertainly. "Who can tell? Maybe she or Chuck has already told someone else at church, or your parents have told. It'd be hard to know for certain."

"I don't like it when I can't thank the person." Serena bit her lip thoughtfully.

"I know what you mean; but, Serena, just be yourself to whomever you speak with."

"What if I put up an unspecific thank you card on the bulletin board at church?"

"That'd work," Carl agreed. "And, of course, you could mention all this to your parents and express how we feel about the mysterious givers." He walked slowly around the room again as Serena followed, still amazed.

"Are you hungry?" she asked him. "What looks good?" He felt like hot wheat cereal, so Serena heated some for both of them. Then they sat at the table together while water heated in the microwave for tea.

"How did schooling go today?" Carl wondered before spooning up a large mouthful of apple cinnamon farina.

"There wasn't a dull moment," Serena responded honestly, "but the girls worked hard. Joelle got a hundred on her math test. We finished Bible, history, science and health before it was time to clean the rooms. How was your day?"

"Busy," Carl agreed. "The parts were hot today. The company needs a lot more this week. My output was way over rate even with the machine's inserts giving us grief. My supervisor couldn't even figure out the problem. He had to call in a service technician late morning. I worked fast and furious all afternoon to make up for the lost time.

"Then washing dishes here in the restaurant was interesting. Tammy, the friendly, overweight waitress, broke four things tonight. No kidding. She's cheerful about it, but I guess that's what she is known for. I would just clean up the glass and start loading the dishwasher again when I'd hear another crash."

The microwave beeped, and Serena turned in her chair toward the small counter. She pulled out the ceramic mug she had been sure to keep out when she packed and lowered the tea bag through the steam. It sank slowly into the water, turning it yellowish-brown until it gradually became dark. She scooped it up with a spoon and carefully yet firmly wrapped the string around it, squeezing it.

"Chris came into the kitchen to talk with me before he went home today," Carl said in between bites. "He asked me how you manage so well with your workload? I admitted that you work harder than I do, and I told him that we are Christians and that our daughters' lives matter more to you than a lucrative career."

Smiling lovingly, she said, "Thank you, Honey. It works both ways, though. You are willing to do what it takes, too. You could easily say to me, 'Stick the girls in public school and go to work.'"

Carl swallowed a mouthful of cereal and cleared his throat. "Then he asked about...can you guess?"

Serena rolled her eyes. "Socialization."

"You got it. I explained to him how that very word is probably the most asked question. I told him the analogy of a greenhouse. Young plants are like our impressionable children. They need time to be sheltered within the home where they learn independent thinking rather than undesirable, oftentimes destructive peer dependency. I told him that you had been home educated and believe you've been better equipped to relate to all age groups now as an adult.

"I even mentioned I Corinthians 15:33. 'Be not deceived: evil communications corrupt good manners.' Then I said that our girls also participate in group lessons through a support group. Ultimately they accept our Biblical values over indoctrination in secular humanism."

"What did he say to all that?" Serena asked.

Carl wiped his mouth with a napkin before answering. "Well, he acted like he was thinking it over. Then he asked about the legality of home schooling. I reminded him about our Constitutional rights to liberty and privacy under the Fourteenth

Amendment as well as the free exercise of religion under the First Amendment that guarantee parents the right to educate their children according to their convictions. I kindly explained, too, that home education is always more affordable than a private school and that we are able to have so much fun time with our girls that we would miss otherwise.

"He seemed to grasp my full meaning because he said, 'Whenever I see your wife working, she's hard at it. Your daughters seem to follow suit. They're always diligently studying or stopping momentarily to assist Serena. I wish my kids knew how to work like that without resting every five minutes and whining.'

"'That's exactly it!' I commended him. Parental teaching is a way of life where the home becomes the center of learning like it has been for centuries in many countries."

Serena had a far away look as she answered, "Home schooling is a way of life that's indomitable and filled with pioneer spirit."

Serena and the girls had just finished breakfast one morning when Suzanne Patton called. "Hello!" her voice sang out through the receiver. "Am I catching you at a bad time, Miss Serena?"

"No, this is a perfect time. I'm usually out of the room all afternoon."

Cheerfully, Suzanne continued, "Maybe this comes as no surprise to you, but I have good news. Jim and I are engaged."

Serena responded with a squeal and exclaimed, "Congratulations, Suzanne! What wonderful news!"

"The date is set for July 19th, and we were wondering if you'd do us the honors of playing the organ or piano for the ceremony. Jim said to tell you that we'd pay for your entire trip. My parents would love to have you stay at the house, too. We don't need an answer right away, so take your time deciding. We'd also be thrilled if your twins would be our flower girls and Carl one of the groomsmen. Resurrection Sunday is fast approaching, so there should be a selection of pretty dresses in the stores. I won't mind at all if you choose them yourselves. You have beautiful, modest taste. Once you find something, let us know the amount; and we'll send you the money."

The girls had overheard Suzanne's excited voice, so they could barely concentrate on Bible and science that morning. All afternoon while Serena vacuumed hotel rooms and heard the girls' lessons, she was preoccupied as well. Suzanne had told of the modern 1600 square foot modular home they had put a down payment on.

Suzanne's parents were conferring a back parcel of their property to them as a wedding gift. The setting would be private since the land had frontage on another road, and trees would hide the two homes from view.

Serena thought of the ease her young friend would have settling a new home that wouldn't need to be painted or cleaned. She tried to rejoice for Suzanne, but she had a difficult time casting down her covetous thoughts. Jim's former in-laws who were Christians and had been praying for his salvation would pay even a well and septic system in full. They wanted to bless him for his decision to accept Christ and encourage him in his new walk. They welcomed Suzanne into their family with open arms as if she were their daughter.

"I know I'll never take their daughter's place," Suzanne had said, "but I'm grateful that they're allowing me a place of my own. Jim and I will have three sets of parents to visit. I couldn't be happier, Miss Serena. Thank you for your prayers and for witnessing to Jim."

Chapter Eighteen

Serenity in the Lord

Late one Tuesday afternoon, the intercom beeped. Serena asked Brookelle to excuse her as she leaned over her across the bed to answer. "Hello, Serena speaking."

"Good afternoon," the receptionist answered. "You have a visitor here that would like to speak with you."

"Sure," Serena said.

Then she heard Mrs. Barletta's voice. "It's Alice, Serena. I know it's rude of me to pop in on you like this, but I'm not inviting myself up. I just came from the new department store in the mall. They have a fabulous sale going on for dresses right now. I wonder if you'd be game to ride over with me."

"Oh, Alice! How thoughtful of you!" Serena exclaimed. "Please do come up for a few minutes."

Alice was knocking on their door shortly. She looked as fresh as always. Her clothing was pressed and crisp, and a delicate string of pearls adorned her neck. She greeted them pleasantly. "This room is lovely, Serena. You've made it quite a home. I'd love to see the girls' schoolbooks if this is a good time."

"Yes," Serena agreed. "The girls can brush their teeth and comb their hair before we go."

The girls eagerly disappeared into the bathroom while Serena offered Alice a chair at the table. "I'm so glad you came!" she thanked her friend.

"I just hope I'm not going to be in the way when Carl gets home."

"You don't need to worry about that," she assured her. "Carl is working in the restaurant until late. Where's your Timmy?" She set some of the textbooks on the table.

"He and Charlie are enjoying a men's night. Charlie ordered a pizza, and they're going to take a walk and read oodles of books. Then they're planning to build a magnificent fort out of fun dough. They told me that they'd leave it up for me to see when I get home. They won't mind since they want it to dry out anyway. Then it will be more permanent for daily play with Timmy's toy soldiers."   Alice's eyes were fixed on the books. She reached for a colorful reader and flipped through its pages with increasing amazement. "You were right! The artwork is fantastic!"

On the way to the store, Alice said, "I hope you don't mind my barging into your plans, but I'm drawn to the girls' section in nearly every store I shop in since you mentioned the upcoming wedding. These are the prettiest ones I've seen yet without going into an actual bridal shop."

The girls took turns holding Alice's and Serena's hands as they walked in.   When they reached the racks of satiny dresses, Alice's eyes sparkled as she said, "Here they are."

Serena gasped at the one Alice held up. "It is gorgeous!" She studied its details. "You have good taste, Alice." The simplicity of the small gown seemed to accentuate the wide, shiny waistband, the puffed sleeves and the double layer of shimmering ruffles around the hem. "That looks like the perfect size, too. I hope there are two of them."

As they slid the hangers on the metal rod, Serena was even surer that dear Alice had selected the best and attractively modest style. There was only the one, but Joelle managed to find a larger size. Alice wondered about using a fitting room. If Serena and the girls still liked them as much after trying them on, would they allow her to purchase them and do the honors of paying a trusted seamstress to take the larger one in?

Serena was taken aback. "You are very kind, but we can buy them. Anyway, Suzanne promised that they'd pay once we let them know the total."

Alice shook her head. "I would be happy to know that I had been able to choose them and purchase them. I may never have that privilege again."

Serena hugged her tightly. "I'll gratefully allow you to get the tights and hair clips, but I just can't accept your offer. Your help in selecting the dresses has been a great help. Feel free to think of Joelle and Brookelle as your adopted daughters for this occasion if you wish."

Alice squeezed her in return. "Okay, but only if you'll permit me to buy their shoes, too." Her eyes squinted mischievously.

The girls wrapped their arms around her waist and looked up at her with broad grins. "Thank you, Mrs. Barletta!"

On July eighteenth, Carl drove their packed car onto the highway. As the station wagon picked up speed, Serena sighed in relief. "We're on our way. This already feels like a family vacation knowing that we'll have you with us for three days straight."

Carl nodded. His brown eyes glowed with understanding. The girls held onto their snacks and drinks Carl had bought for them when he had filled the gas tank. After three hours, they crossed the Ohio line. They were pleased with their progress in spite of stopping every hour as Serena's doctor had advised for her to stretch her legs. Serena called the Pattons on the cell phone to let them know how they were doing time-wise and when to expect them.

The driving was nicer in Ohio. The highway smoothed out and sounded quieter beneath the tires' tread. Three and a half hours later, Carl turned off the black four lanes onto asphalt. The farmers' fields that surrounded the road were flat and lined with trees against the horizon. The sun pulsated earnestly as it slowly descended toward its evening position. The countryside wasn't as breathtaking as the hills of New York, but it was where people that they loved dearly in the Lord lived. That made the lush green seem sufficient for Serena's travel weary body. One more turn and they were on the Patton's gravel road.

Carl pulled slowly into their driveway, and they sat there looking at the house. "Thank You for a safe trip, Lord," Carl prayed aloud. He opened his door, and they all followed suit. The breeze was as vigorous as it always was across the open yards and fields surrounding them. The blood pulsated a little less sluggishly through Serena's bulging, bruised veins.

Mrs. Patton welcomed them in cordially and urged them to eat the meal she had prepared before they all must leave for the rehearsal. She bent down to hug the girls and exclaimed over how much they had grown over the past year. "Suzanne and Mr. Patton had to run some last minute errands. They'll meet us there." Suzanne's brothers sat down with them, teasing the girls as if they were younger sisters. Joelle and Brookelle enjoyed it all, unaccustomed to the jollity of brothers.

The Romaine salad, layered with thawed peas, cheddar cheese and bacon, tasted fresh and light after sitting for so long in the car and snacking on crackers for lunch. Serena only ate half of a grilled chicken breast, opting for more salad to satisfy her. Then Carl brought in their fresh changes of clothing, and Serena smoothed the girls' hair again.

The church members that were taking part in the wedding were all happy to see Carl and Serena reunited with their twin daughters. Nearly everyone made some comment about their heights and darker hair shades.

Soon Serena was taking her place at the piano. She felt as if she'd absorbed into the lovely bridesmaids' processional. The Grand had been moved across the stage beside the organ, so she could scoot over to play the "Bridal Chorus" majestically in full sound as well as the "Wedding March" at the end.

Suzanne commended the twins and Serena as they descended the basement stairs for the rehearsal snack and dessert buffet. "You girls were like pros walking down the aisle, and you played the music smoothly with feeling...like always. Jim and I just had to have you; and, of course we're thrilled to have Mr. Callahan be a groomsman. Stephen is out of town this weekend, too; so we wouldn't have been able to choose this date if it weren't for you. This was the only free weekend some of Jim's relatives had this entire month." She squeezed her fiancé's arm, and he awarded her a handsome smile.

Then, looking at Carl, Jim asked, "Was the check I sent you adequate enough for your expenses? I brought cash with me to pay the difference if it wasn't."

Carl gently slapped him on the back. "More than enough, Brother in Christ."

Serena grasped the railing on the last step as an unexpected contraction seized her. His family met Jim and Suzanne, so they were jostled toward the tables with them. Carl stood on the white tiled floor, holding each girl's hand. He turned back toward Serena and asked, "Are you ready to find a place to sit?" When he saw her tight lips, his eyebrows furrowed in concern. "Serena, are you all right?"

She managed to nod as the tightening eased and whispered, "I believe I just had a Braxton-Hicks contraction. Don't be alarmed. I don't want anyone to know." She released the railing and stepped down beside Joelle. "I'll just put my feet up on a chair and drink some water. Maybe that will inhibit more."

Carl found a table against the wall where Serena could be discreet before he went to get a cup of water. He returned with a fluffy biscuit covered with mashed, sugary strawberries and whipped cream. He went back up with the girls for their own selections and was stopped by Jim who wanted to introduce him to his family and former in-laws. Shortly, his mother-in-law and sister-in-law approached Serena and thanked her for her part in preparing Jim's heart for salvation. "We have been praying ever since we found the Lord that Jim would accept Christ as well. He is so peaceful now," the older woman said.

The sister added, "And Suzanne has made him very happy. She's beautiful!" She gazed at her silky, cascading hair before shaking Serena's hand warmly. "It's been a pleasure to meet you."

Suzanne told Serena and Carl back at the house that she insisted they sleep in her double bed. She'd be perfectly comfortable on the family room couch. Joelle and Brookelle excitedly rolled out their sleeping bags on the plush carpeting at the foot of the bed. Once they had brushed their teeth and slipped into their pajamas, they hurried back to Suzanne's room and willingly crawled into them.

Carl prayed with all four of them, specifically asking God to hold off the baby's arrival until after the wedding. Serena had only felt one more contraction in the car coming back from church. "I think a good night's sleep will keep them at bay, Lord willing," she said.

Her feet glided on the quality sheets as she slid between them. "Wow!" she exclaimed in a loud whisper. "I'm not used to this high thread count. I feel like I'm floating on a cloud."

The morning of the wedding day was drizzly, but the birds still greeted the day melodiously. Serena nervously climbed out of bed. She thanked God silently for a good night's sleep and asked Him again to help her through the wedding for Jim and Suzanne's sake. She encouraged herself that at least the occasion wasn't to be in the evening. She only had to make it through several hours.

However, the longer she was on her feet, her belly began tightening again. This time she felt discomfort in her back that radiated around to the front. It had been a while since the twins' births, but she was certain her real labor had felt this way. She helped the girls roll up their sleeping bags before returning to the bed. She told Carl, "I think I should stay in bed as long as I can with my knees bent up to prevent this baby from interrupting the wedding."

Carl looked at her apprehensively, but he quickly took the girls down to the kitchen. Serena heard the Patton boys' cheerful voices and laughter responding to Carl's pleasant "Good morning." Serena found herself wishing for a baby boy to add liveliness to their home as well. Then the warm scent of toasting bagels wafted up the steps, but Serena didn't feel hungry. She only longed for a cup of hot tea.

When they came back upstairs, Carl set Serena's curling iron on the nightstand and plugged it in for her. Serena washed her face with cleansing wipes before applying her makeup while the iron heated. Still sitting in bed, she managed to curl her hair. The dresser mirror was large enough that she could see from the bed.

Then she cautiously headed into the bathroom to freshen up and brush her teeth. She slipped into her dress without mussing her hair. She had wanted to take a shower, but she didn't dare stand that long. She was glad she had soaked in the tub at home the day before and had made sure the girls were thorough with their baths.

All of the Pattons had left by the time Carl walked the girls out to the car, carrying the bag with Serena's music and the twins' brushes and hairspray. The stylist Suzanne had hired would be busy on the other ladies' updos in the large restroom at the church, so they weren't in a rush. Carl returned to the house to escort Serena out. "Serena, I'm feeling uncomfortable with you having to accompany this wedding in your condition."

"Please," Serena pleaded, "How can I back out so suddenly?"

"I know," Carl said compassionately. "Who would have thought you'd go into labor being several weeks early?"

"At least my water has never broken on its own before," Serena tried to assure themselves, "and my labor usually lasts a good seven hours."

Carl nodded and opened the passenger door.

As it neared one o'clock, the regular contractions were becoming stronger. They were still fifteen minutes apart, but Serena prayed earnestly that she'd get through the ceremony. Joelle and Brookelle were little princesses with their halo-type French braids and softly curled tendrils that softened their exuberant faces. Wisps of Babies' Breath adorned the swooped hair where it tucked into the upbraids. The stylist even sprayed a modest amount of sparkle hairspray over the final hairdos. "You girls are pictures of femininity," Serena said.

Another dull ache began to wrap around her back and waist, and she felt a lot more pressure in her varicose veins than she normally did. She clenched her teeth discreetly, hoping no one noticed her ease onto the clean white linoleum floor where she could stretch her legs out in front of her. She managed a smile when anyone looked her way, hoping she seemed nonchalant. The flowery clock confirmed that it was 12:30 and time for her to play the prelude. As soon as that contraction eased, she held her hands out to her girls with another smile. They helped her up, and she kissed them. "You'll do a great job. I love you."

Serena stopped to talk with Carl at the sanctuary's double doors. "You look so handsome in your tux, Honey. I'm glad Jim asked you to be usher and groomsman."

Carl's smile showed his pearly white teeth. The entire wedding party were wearing white. His dark hair and eyes were a striking contrast.

"The girls are all ready, too; so I'm ready to begin the music." Carl opened the door for her, and she took one step before a hard contraction seized her. She stood still and clenched her teeth. Carl had been watching her through the door's window and hurried in. Holding her arm, he led her to the nearest pew. When he could tell her pain was temporarily eased, he asked, "It's the real thing isn't it?"

Serena nodded. "If only the baby will hold off until the ceremony's over. I need to get up to the piano before the guests begin to arrive."

Carl wrapped his strong arm around her while she leaned on his other hand. He kissed her forehead as she eased onto the bench. "I'll be up to get you as soon as the recessional's over."

"But, Carl, they'll need you to usher..." she spoke to his retreating form as he hurried back toward the lobby. She knew he meant business. Halfway through "O Perfect Love", another groomsman ushered a family in. Serena willed her fingers to stroke the keys calmly; but as she was concluding "Walk Hand in Hand with Me," the baby's pressure grew intense. Her thighs ached, and politely adjusting her position on the bench didn't ease the pain. She was trying so hard to suppress it that her fingers began to shake.

Thankfully she had practiced enough at church in New York that the sound still floated out smoothly. She didn't look out at the people now, because she sensed that the auditorium was nearly full by the hum of voices and blur of colors she saw in her peripheral vision. Her watch was propped on the music rack in a visible place. After playing Pachelbel's "Canon in D" for the mothers of the bride and groom, the hands on its face confirmed that it was one o'clock. She glanced back at the doors to be sure the bridesmaids were ready before she began "Fairest Lord Jesus."

When the third modest young lady had reached the platform's steps, Serena slowed the arpeggios to a graceful ending and hobbled the two steps to the organ bench. She had preset the registrations and turned the large instrument on to warm up when she had briefly practiced that morning. She only had to pull the pedal drawbars once she was situated, so she wouldn't accidentally be sounding the bass notes as she stepped onto the pedals to sit down.

Her music was ready, so she tenderly sounded out the early part of the "Bridal Chorus" while the twins came. As they neared the front, she gradually pressed the volume pedal with her toes into a crescendo and sounded the notes loudly and clearly. Suzanne seemed to glide down the aisle on nothing but her dad's arm. She seemed unashamed of her luminous smile as she stared ahead at no one besides Jim. Serena played ritardando as Suzanne came to a stop. Then she reached the last three chords that she played in double time.

The vows, song, and candle lighting proceeded smoothly until the ring exchanges. Suzanne struggled to slide Jim's wedding band over his knuckle. After attempting twice, her cheeks flushed. Pastor Eclant said, "That ring sure won't be coming off." Everyone laughed while Jim calmly finished wriggling it on with a reassuring smile. Every muscle in Serena's body tensed, as she fought to hold off the labor a little longer. Pastor finally announced the new husband and wife as they turned to face the crowd. Serena played the triplets and dotted half notes of the "Wedding March" with gusto. Then as the attendants met, in turn, at the center of the platform to go out together, she softened the sound with the volume pedal.

Carl looked at her questioningly as he walked toward his escort in turn. Serena nodded slightly, with raised eyebrows and urgency in her blue eyes. Carl walked faster than the others had and was soon racing around the side of the auditorium toward her while the groomsmen came back in to dismiss the rows. "We're leaving NOW!" Carl demanded.

Serena abruptly stopped the romantic postlude music and reached up to push the drawbars back in and turn the organ off.

"NOW!" Carl persisted. "Someone else will have to figure all that out. We've waited long enough. Mrs. Patton is calling an ambulance."

"An ambulance?" Serena squeaked, but as she stiffly got off the bench, she felt a gush of warm water. In horrified embarrassment, she stared down at her soaked feet and then at Carl.

Without a moment's hesitation, he scooped her up into his arms and rushed toward the back. All Serena could think of then was the urge to push. She concentrated hard on restraining, but the feeling was almost uncontrollable. She heard gasps and the immediate hush that fell over the crowd, yet she felt like she were an onlooker herself. The entire thing seemed like she were dreaming. Thankfully, the ambulance was there within minutes. The paramedics took her and eased her onto the stretcher. As they wheeled it up the ramp, she thought she heard Carl somewhere in the background saying, "I'll meet you at the hospital, Honey!"

The driver shut the doors, someone was pulling the window curtains, and a soothing female voice was soon saying, "The baby's ready, Ma'am. You don't need to fight anymore. Relax and focus on seeing your little one momentarily."

When Carl reached the hospital, the admissions staff could only tell him that Serena was still out in the ambulance. His face grew pale, and they hastened to assure him that everything was under control and that they'd let him know as soon as she was wheeled into a room. He paced the glossy floor and mouthed fervent prayers. After the longest half hour ever, a tired nurse called him, almost rudely. "Carl Callahan?"

He almost had to run to follow her down the hallway. Then the grumpy RN abruptly turned into a room and stood just inside the door. Once he entered, she hastily left. Nervously, Carl proceeded in. A dim light was on behind the privacy divider, and he heard hushed voices. As he hesitated, a stranger's female voice spoke his name. He answered apprehensively, "Yes?" Then he saw her familiar face at the foot of the bed.   He didn't dare peek around the divider.

"I'm Sharon," she introduced herself. Nodding toward the head of the bed, she said, "I cared for your wife on the ambulance. She's a brave lady, and you both have a beautiful baby. Congratulations!"

Then he turned and saw Serena's contented smile and a small fuzzy head resting in the crook of her arm, its swaddled form hidden beneath her sheet. "Come and see little Joseph Allegro," she said sweetly. Looking up to thank the paramedics, Serena saw that they had already gone.

Carl sat down gingerly by her legs and gazed gratefully into her eyes. "I was so worried about you. Thank you for bearing me a son, 'Rena." Then he lifted the tiny bundle into his arms. "*Allegro* after *Allegra*. I like that," he commended. "Tomorrow I'll stop by Allegra's grave." Studying Joseph's red, wrinkled face, he said, "He sure has a masculine look, doesn't he?"

Serena nodded happily. "Carl, where are Joelle and Brookelle?"

"Mrs. Patton promised that she wouldn't let them out of her sight. They're probably done with the pictures by now and at the reception."

"Oh, Carl, you won't be in any of the pictures," Serena worried.

"Are you kidding?" Carl asked incredulously. "You know how I can't stand having my picture taken. Anyway, the reason behind my absence will always be a reminder of the unique situation. Jim and Suzanne will never forget little Joseph's birthday! You should know by now that I love you more than anyone else in the world."

The two days that Serena and Joseph spent in Kettering Hospital were joyful. Joelle and Brookelle were doting big sisters, and the newlyweds called from their hotel to congratulate and thank them and make sure all was well. Mrs. Patton held baby Joseph and assured Serena that having the girls around the house helped fill some of the emptiness without Suzanne. Serena had promised Jerusha a few months earlier that she would phone her with the news. Jerusha was thrilled and told her what an answer he was to her prayers. She must have called the Huffs herself, because they all came bringing Dan with them.

Claire and Blaire had grown considerably and looked more like young ladies than preschoolers. They held back at first, but when Serena held out her arms to them, they rushed forward. She gripped them tightly and looked past their heads expecting to see haughty jealousy in Miss Emili's eyes, but there was none. She sensed a change in both Mr. and Mrs. Huff. Smiles lit both of their faces, and Dan stood blindly staring into the emptiness he now saw due to glaucoma and macular degeneration. Tears began to spill from Serena's eyes as she introduced them all to her family. She placed Carl's hand in Dan's wrinkled one. Dan wrapped his other hand warmly around his.

Joelle and Brookelle copied Carl's, "It's nice to meet you," while smiling sincerely. Carl was holding the baby and bent down to allow the girls a closer look. "Feel his grip already, Blaire," he said. "If you'll sit down in the rocking chair over there, Claire, I'll allow you girls to take turns holding Joseph." He knelt beside the chair, guarding the baby's head and neck with his large hand.

Miss Emili approached the bed then. "I'm glad the Lord allowed you to have the baby here so we'd have the opportunity to talk with you in person. Mr. Huff and I can't thank you enough for all that you've done for our family."

Mr. Huff nodded in agreement.

Emili continued, "Our girls missed you terribly after you moved. The topics you had discussed and the fun you showed them during the time you were their nanny was all they could talk about. At first, I admit, I was envious. Then I began to realize that we all make choices in life.

You weren't trying to make me jealous. You were simply having a relationship with my girls that I should have had. I had been choosing wealth over my family, but I longed for the bond you had with them and the one you were establishing with your own twins again in New York.

"I struggled mentally for a while about quitting my job and staying home, but I couldn't bear the thought of giving up my extravagant lifestyle. Our neighbor, your friend Bethany, threw a party two months ago. As an outsider in her home, my eyes were completely opened for the first time. She seemed like a facade. The real her was hidden behind a costume of perfect manners, lovely belongings, and delectable foods. She almost bragged about her carefree life without the hindrances of children.

Her husband didn't seem happy at all, and there seemed to be an invisible wall of politeness between them. There was only surface happiness with all the neighbors, too; so it seemed. I realized that I was also hoping to be recognized and have my gown noticed. Everyone remembered the last party with your piano entertainment and was discreetly talking about how they could outdo her romanticism at their events.

"I left feeling discouraged about the direction my life was taking. I didn't want to end up the same way. Belongings and prestige are no exchange for people who truly love you. My husband was in perfect agreement, actually relieved, when I discussed my findings with him. Dan really needs my help, too, since Barb passed away. We shop more frugally, and I type medical transcriptions at home in the evenings when Mr. Huff is home to play with the girls."

"So you are teaching the girls then?" Serena wanted to be sure.

"Absolutely," Mr. Huff said, looking at Emili with admiration. "Our lives have never been better."

"There were things I had to adjust to at first...but, Serena," Emili concluded, "the biggest change in our lives took place when we read the tract you gave us at Christmas. At first, it made us angry. We were good, responsible people. Those Bible verses, however, worked on us. Barb explained what it all meant from her hospital bed since she had become a Christian. We're attending your old church now, and Dan rides along with us just to be there and pray for the services since he can't know what's taking place."

Turning toward Carl, Serena asked for the baby. She held him close as she stood on the floor in her modest, feminine pajamas and robe Mrs. Shelby had bought and presented to her the evening before. Placing a hand on Dan's shoulder, she alerted him to her nearness. She briefly leaned her head against the grandfatherly shoulder before stroking his baby soft cheek.

Mr. Huff explained gruffly, "Dan still shaves himself by feeling carefully with his fingers. He smells so good...like normal."

In spite of his condition like Helen Keller's, he stood there peacefully in accepting surrender. Serena took his hand lovingly in hers and placed it on Joseph's head. Tenderly, the man began to feel with his fingertips. He felt of the tiny nose, the smooth forehead and cheeks. He gingerly placed one of the small hands on his own and warmed it with his other. Then he kissed the infant's fingertips before speaking as clearly as he could without being able to hear himself. "Congra-du-lations, Serena. I prayed fo- yo- twins. Are they here with you? May I see them?"

Carl ushered the girls around the bed, and Serena smiled encouragingly. "Dan is a dear man, Girls. Don't be afraid."

The elderly man stroked the girls' healthy, clean hair and enunciated, "You have wonde-ful parents, and yo-- mom is a dear. She helped my wife after her surgery by taking her, in her spare time, to buy groceries and even helped do extra chores at the Huffs' house to ease her workload for a while. I know, though, that your mom missed you girls terribly. I could see the pain in her eyes. Always know, though," he labored slowly, "that because of your separation, my wife and I got saved...and the Huffs. Your family will reap rewards in Heaven."

Serena couldn't hold back the new wave of tears any longer. Before they left, Dan patted up Serena's arm until he reached her face. He felt her wet cheeks and squeezed her other hand. Then he spoke again, but Serena couldn't make out his words.

Emili interpreted, "He says that he'll continue praying for you and your family every day, and he loves you in the Lord."

Serena hoped for visits from Bethany and Jerusha, but they never came or called. The day she and the baby were to be discharged, Carl and the girls packed up at the Pattons' and came to the hospital ready to leave for New York.

Carl hadn't worked at the machine shop long enough to have personal days or vacation time, but his supervisor was gracious enough to give him the extra days off without pay when Carl had phoned him. He'd be expected at work first thing the next morning. As they traveled, the baby slept well in the car seat Carl had bought.   He had given Joelle and Brookelle three models to choose from that were in the lower price bracket and allowed them to decide for him. The infant seat was covered with light blue material, dotted with navy blue stars and pale yellow stripes.

The motherly sisters took turns reading library books to their oblivious brother while Serena prayed silently. She had so much to thank God for, and somehow she actually looked forward to returning to the hotel room. It was home for now...their own spot to kick off their shoes, and it was clean. She also prayed for Bethany and her husband. The girls finally dozed off, and Carl made good time. They were walking into their room in Corning by 8:30 that night.

Having forgotten to turn their cell phone on during the trip, Carl checked it after he unloaded the car. There was one message. It was from their former landlord, Dr. Noyes. He said that the office house wasn't being rented after all. The person had backed out of the deal. The more he had thought about the situation and the economy's housing/mortgaging crisis, he realized he'd be better off working out a permanent arrangement with them. He could trust them, and he was assuming that they'd like the place. If they were willing to consider the offer, he'd like for them to call him. Serena felt chills run up and down her spine when Carl related the voice mail.

They knelt as a family beside their bed, and Carl thanked the Lord for keeping them safe on the trip as well as protecting Serena and Joseph during the labor and delivery. Then Serena prayed, praising Him for having worked in the Huffs' lives and Dan's and Barb's. Even the twins took turns commenting to the Lord about their take on the wedding and their baby brother. Carl concluded their devotion time by asking God to close the housing opportunity if it wasn't His perfect will for them and to give them the wisdom to know the difference.

Once the girls were bedded down and Serena sat down to feed the baby, Carl called both sets of parents asking them for advice. If Carl's parents didn't live so far away, they'd be there to look at the house, too, his dad said. Both dads assured Carl that they'd be earnestly praying for them to have reassuring peace one way or the other. Carl asked Serena's dad to come, and Mom, too, if they were free. They said they'd make the time...just to let them know when.

Serena put Joseph in his bassinet, so they could talk it out as a couple over decaffeinated coffee. They analyzed and figured over the positives and negatives. They would need to know what interest rate Doctor Noyes had in mind. How many years would he mortgage the house for?

What if a better offer suddenly came along? Would he decide to back out? They would want a binding contract so he couldn't refinance to his advantage.

They discussed how they'd continue to be frugal and buy things at yard sales or wait on things that weren't necessities. Serena didn't pick up junk while rummaging...only practical items. She wouldn't buy used cloth furniture--just metal, wicker or plastic that she could clean thoroughly. She'd rather keep on getting by with the air mattresses and uncomfortable futon that were new than bring home something questionable.

Carl praised, "You and the girls were pretty amazing at how beautifully you furnished the apartment over the garage. I know I couldn't have done so well by learning from library books how to repair things. I haven't talked to any man yet whose wife and children don masks to sand and stain old shelving units and dressers."

Serena smiled. "Well, the girls and I were blessed that we happened to be out for a walk after Christmas when people had just replaced their old furniture. Those shelves were solid for the schoolbooks."

"Was it the goodwill store where you found the abused dressers—covered with stickers and spray paint?"

"Yes. It was the furniture sale day, and I got both of them for ten dollars.   The girls and I spent three days and two evenings scraping and washing them before we could sponge paint them pink and purple."

Carl nodded. "Despite the dressers' different fabrications, they looked like they were meant to be a set in the girls' room. The girls are so proud of those dressers. If we get the house, Honey, you could use the garage apartment to teach your piano students...or at least to adequately hostess recitals."

Carl called Doctor Noyes's cell phone the next morning while on break at work and called Serena at lunchtime. "The doctor is up here right now working with his attorney on some things and would like to get back to South Carolina by Wednesday if at all possible. He wondered if we could meet him at 4:30 this evening, so I called The Luxury already and asked Terrell if he'd like some extra hours. He was willing to stay and work an extra shift."

"Great!" Serena agreed. After she hung up, she called Alice Barletta. She was more than willing to babysit. When they arrived, little Timothy opened the door before they could knock, and Alice was sheepishly behind him. Her polite manners couldn't hide the eager look in her eyes to get her hands on the baby. Serena passed the sleeping bundle to her with a warm smile. "I packed supper for the girls, and there's a small bottle of milk I managed to express that should hold Joseph over. Thank you so much, Alice."

They arrived at the office promptly at 4:30. Serena's parents were already standing in the driveway in front of the garage talking with Doctor Noyes and his lawyer.

They all entered the house from the back. Carl had been in the house once when Doctor Noyes was still seeing patients there, but Serena had never seen the inside. One walk through it and Serena was reassured by an overwhelming peace. She could tell that Carl felt the same way, and both her parents' eyes were twinkling.

The floor plan was spacious enough for a cottage style, yet homey. Serena felt like she couldn't have designed it any better herself. Because of the professional purpose the older home had been remodeled for, there was a receptionist greeting area at the front door. Serena could picture in her mind's eye how she'd set a lace doily and candy dish on the stark white counter. Perhaps she'd even find some rustic blue shutters to prop up. A welcome sign and greenery would look hospitable attached to them.

The men decided to study the plumbing, furnace and wiring in the basement, so the women were left alone. Mom said, "Oh, Serena! I like how you'd have a partitioned greeting room like this."

"So do I," Serena said with a contented sigh. "If we happen to have a bad day and the house looks messy, unexpected company won't see everything at a glance."

The two of them took a second tour starting upstairs beneath the slanted roof. There was a large bedroom on one side of the steps that Serena determined would be the master suite. A good-sized dormer allowed the bathroom at the head of the stairs to be boxy and bright. "Carl likes lighthouses, so I'll probably decorate this room with nautical accents over time," Serena commented.

"The blue walls will fit that theme perfectly," Mom noticed.

On the other side of the staircase, there were two more rooms. The first one was tiny with a narrow window. "This would be ideal for storage," Serena thought aloud what she had been silent about when Doctor Noyes and his lawyer had been with them.

As they returned to the hallway and headed toward the back room, the passage suddenly opened up into a nook where it appeared the doctor had kept his personal desk and reference books. Glass doors covered the cases high on the two straight interior walls, and a small frosted crank skylight with a screen was centered in the ceiling that sloped halfway to the floor. There was plenty of room for a single bed in the center of the spot. "This would be ideal for Joseph when he gets older," Serena said. "Being a boy, modesty wouldn't be an issue since he can change in the bathroom; and I can look at clouds with him when I put him down for naps."

The last room off the nook was big enough for the girls to have bunk beds. She mentally figured where she would put the dressers and a wardrobe. There would just be enough space.

Back downstairs, they walked through the cafe doors that swung into the light-filled kitchen in the back of the house. A large window over the sink would enable Serena to watch the children play in the small fenced-in yard that the girls had enjoyed when they had lived in the apartment. A large trampoline and swing set would fit comfortably.

Mom said, "I've always liked the tall white picket fencing rather than chain link. It's much prettier and safer for the children since people can't easily climb it." There were neighbors on every side, but they were all pleasant and helpful. The months they had lived over the garage, they had kept to themselves for the most part. Serena liked feeling looked out for anyway instead of being hidden in some remote location. She anticipated baking pies for them if they did become official residents.

After the men found them, they all decided to go to The Luxury's restaurant for lunch while reading over the documents the doctor's attorney had printed up. Serena's parents didn't have any qualms about the terms' wording, so Carl decided to go ahead and meet with their own lawyer on lunch break the next day before he signed. The doctor agreed to meet him there.

Serena had devotions with the children the next morning like normal. They prayed extra hard about the house. The girls liked the thought of being back where it had begun to feel like home. Summer was the perfect time to move. Before they cleaned the other rooms, they made their own beds, wiped down the bathroom, and tied up the garbage bag. Serena was feeding the baby before snuggling him into his carrier when Jerusha called.

"Hello, Serena dear. How are you and the baby doing? I wished I could have visited you in the hospital before you left Ohio. I was so busy helping Bethany then that I couldn't get away. I can hardly believe I'm calling you like this, but please be honest with me. Promise?"

"I'll be honest," Serena said, wonderingly.

"Well, the Jasmines are divorcing. Bethany isn't willing to have children, so her husband has left her. Bethany doesn't want to stay in the house and has decided to make a drastic change. She's moving to Italy to live with her grandfather for the time being. I guess there's an open position in a clinic there that she's excited about filling."

"What are you going to do?" Serena asked while she lifted Joseph up to pat his back.

"I'm awkward to suggest this, so I'll rush through it. I'm wondering if you could use a housekeeper, occasional nanny, gardener, and helper with teaching Joelle and Brookelle? I'd pay rent if I could just have a corner to sleep on a cushioned cot with a curtain to pull for privacy. You are like a daughter to me, Serena. You know that. You've told me how pleasant the area is up there, and you know how awful Dayton can be. I've never enjoyed big cities."

Everyone was excited that they would be in their own place again. A city home would seem much more private than a hotel residence. They'd finally be able to laugh out loud again even if it were late at night. The packing seemed like a fun chore this time. Serena felt giddy just knowing that she'd only be responsible for her own house again...no more cleaning hotel rooms.

They were up before dawn on moving day. Hurriedly they stripped the beds' linens, putting back on the hotel's sheets and coverlets.   They gulped down cold cereal. All around them there were packed boxes and bulging suitcases. Once they had all brushed their teeth and Serena had smoothed the girls' hair into thick ponytails, they finished stowing everything into the toiletry duffel bag. With the diaper bag in hand, Carl locked up and led them all into the elevator and out to the car.

Serena followed him as he drove the rental truck and soon pulled into Serena's parents' driveway to get their furniture and other stored items. Serena parked closer to the road, so she wouldn't be in the way. Then the girls spotted Jim and Dad coming out of the garage lugging a bookshelf. Chuck Barletta followed close behind with three stacked boxes. Suzanne came rushing out of the house's side door. Serena got out of the car to give her hug.

"Thank you so much for bringing Jerusha up to live with us."

Jerusha came out more slowly with Mom and Alice on either side of her. "Jerusha!" Serena squealed. The two of them laughed merrily as they embraced.

Carl asked Jim, "How's married life treating you two?"

"Just like yours is treating you," he replied jovially, nodding toward little Joseph still buckled in his car seat. His eyes danced playfully.

"Congratulations, you two!" Carl and Serena exclaimed.

The new couple beamed at their response. "We were kind of hoping that you'd allow our child to call you 'Aunt' and 'Uncle' since you are our brother and sister in Christ," Jim queried.

"That would be great!" Carl agreed. "On one condition, though. May our children call you the same?"

"Yes! We'd be delighted!" Suzanne gushed enthusiastically. "Please have them call me 'Aunt Ellie' after my middle name Eleanor. I've thought about how your girls and I share a name form. We all have 'ele' in our names. Did you know that's French for light and warm-hearted?"

"I believe it--the way you are," Serena said, squeezing her hand.

"Today is a day of surprises," Suzanne hinted.

The twins stared through the open window...their eyes large and wondering.

Jim rubbed his hands together excitedly. "Since Dan has moved in with the Huffs now that he's completely blind and deaf, you've inherited all his household furnishings. He and Barbara never had any children, and their will made it very clear that you should receive it as soon as they no longer had use of it all."

The girls clapped their hands, and Carl whooped. "God is so good!"

Serena looked down at their healthy son sleeping peacefully in his bassinet in their settled bedroom. Carl stood beside her, his hand on her shoulder. "Won't be long, and he'll need to move out to his crib."

Serena grimaced playfully. "That's a mixed blessing," she retorted, chuckling softly. "Little Joseph will be a constant reminder of how the accounts of Joseph in the Bible encouraged me during our valley experiences. It's funny, Carl. Now that those times are past, it makes this moment more precious than ever." She turned to put her arms around Carl and leaned her head on his chest. "I hope Allegra can see from the Cloud of Witnesses that I named him after her because we love her so much."

Carl nodded. He squeezed her closer. "I'm sure Allegra is rooting for us to train him up in the way he should go so that he'll have the character Joseph had to do right no matter what."

"Well, he will then."

Carl looked at her.

"He will because he has a father like you who also does right no matter what. You could have easily filed bankruptcy like so many people do, but you faced your commitments head on." She spoke with fervency.

"The same goes for you, too, then. Serena, I have so much to thank you for. You've communicated such loyalty and acceptance toward me when I created such turmoil for our family and tried your best to focus on the positive side of things. You always dress beautifully with the meager clothes you've had to work with and make yourself pretty for me. You've represented me well as your provider. Do you remember how you struggled when Merry and Dominic were in the limelight at church?"

"Yes," Serena admitted sadly. "That was only because of my selfish pride that I let it bother me. I missed Merry's companionship a lot, but still that was no excuse to be bitter or envious of her."

"Right, and I know you pray earnestly for Merry and Dominic. What I'm getting at, though, is the fact that maybe one of our own children will go to the mission field someday because you didn't give up during our difficulties. Your rewards will be just as precious in Heaven to you as our child's rewards are to him or her. You've sacrificed today so that you may reap rewards tomorrow. You've invested in people rather than choosing a career. We've already seen some fruits from your labors…

like our Ohioan friends. I'm honored to have you for my wife. You've taught me so much and made me look good when any other woman would have left me."

Feet pattering on the steps stopped in the doorway. "Nana Jerusha said that I may come in to get my bunny," Brookelle explained breathlessly, "'cause Bunny wouldn't want to miss our slumber party. He prob'ly remembers sleeping in the apartment with me." Then she hurried down the hall. As she ran back toward the stairs, she called out, "We're going to make toffee popcorn and read stories!" She couldn't seem to race downstairs fast enough.

"It's still a miracle that they're back with us, isn't it?" Carl said.

Serena nodded fervently.

It does my heart good, Serena," Carl said with startling heartfelt gruffness, "to see how God has even blessed you with a helper that's a dear family member now after all the hard work and humiliation you endured. I know there was a lot that took place that most of our acquaintances never knew...or forgot about and haven't had to experience themselves. That's the amazing thing about God. In spite of this earthly life not being fair, He sets things straight...if not here, then in Heaven."

Serena stood still in overwhelmed silence.

Carl broke it by asking, "How about getting a snack ourselves and watching our wedding video?"

"Yes." Serena's voice was wobbly. "Thank you, Carl, for such a good grade on your verbal 'report card' to me."

"'Honour to whom honour is due'," he quoted.

"I thank God everyday for you, Carl," she said sincerely. "By following your leadership and staying close to the Lord, I've learned what it's like to experience serenity through the poorer side of our vows."

"How fitting," Carl mused, "You spoke of Joseph's name and what it means to you. What about yours? Serena...Serena's Serenity?"